W9-AQN-045

DATE DUE			
MAR 6			
DEC 11			

60334
Gaiani

St. Procopius College Library
Maple Ave. & College Rd.
Lisle, Illinois

FOR A BETTER RELIGIOUS LIFE

FOR A BETTER RELIGIOUS LIFE

P. Vitus Gaiani, O.F.M.

Translated by

Rev. Father Patrick, O.S.B.

WITHDRAWN

ST. PAUL PUBLICATIONS

NEW YORK - DETROIT - BOSTON

255
G-12f

NIHIL OBSTAT:
   The Rt. Rev. Msgr. Merwin Lenk, D.D.
      Censor Librorum

IMPRIMATUR:
   The Rt. Rev. Msgr. Bernard Kearns
      Vicar General of Detroit

November 14, 1962

Library of Congress Catalogue Card Number: 62-20956

Copyright 1962 by The Society of St. Paul, Staten Island 14, N.Y.
Printed in U.S.A. by The Society of St. Paul, Staten Island 14, N.Y.

60334

CONTENTS

II   THE STATE OF PERFECTION

III   THE THREE EVANGELICAL COUNSELS

IV RELIGIOUS POVERTY

V RELIGIOUS OBEDIENCE

XII   ADAPTATION OF THE RELIGIOUS LIFE

PREFACE

The *International Congress of the States of Perfection* was held in Rome during the Holy Year and the Report of the discussions, which filled four large volumes, appeared recently. The English-speaking world has had to await many years this digest of the Report in translation. Feeling that it would not be probable that the entire Report would be read by all religious, or even by the majority of them, *Father Gaiani* has taken the key considerations and grouped them together into this handy, more concise form.

The author was careful to include all the essential ascetical and theological aspects of religious life, as well as those of particular interest to English-speaking persons. The book, therefore, has considerations about the fundamental concept of the "state of perfection" as such, the vows, mortification, religious humility, the common life, and all the other means toward religious perfection.

The decision was made to limit the subject matter to the religious life, considered in itself, in its essential, ascetical and theological aspects, and in the means of perfection that it offers to consecrated souls. But even this one subject cannot be treated here exhaustively. The main aim of the Congress—to treat of the external and internal life of the religious—is necessarily reflected in this digest, but is limited in its development by the number of pages at our disposal.

The chief interest of this book is its wonderful timeliness in presenting a plan for religious perfection in our twentieth century. Older treatises just did not contemplate such problems as those raised by movies' and television's influence on religious life, or by the modern preoccupation with comfort. These and many more most timely subjects are carefully considered, without either departing excessively from traditional views or veering off into the quasi-heresy of "the new for newness' sake."

The subjects are here set forth in such a way that consecrated souls can derive solid and genuine food, a clear light to guide them, and a deep warmth capable of exciting in their hearts generous and genuine love of God and neighbor. Hence the title: *For a Better Religious Life.*

Interest in this digest flows from the following facts:

1) It synthesizes the thought of numerous learned and pious men, most of whom are in religion. These are people differing in nationality, mentality and occupation, who belong to various Congregations and who have been chosen or consulted by the Sacred Congregation of Religious.

2) The discourses and writings of these men, corresponding to the subjects proposed or approved by the same Congregation, were examined and, with the consent of the authors, corrected, lengthened or shortened by a special commission of religious.

3) They fill four large volumes and are published under the title, *Acta et Documenta Congressus Generalis de*

statibus perfectionis, having been edited by the Society of St. Paul. (Edizioni Paoline, Rome).

The method followed in our present work is equally distant from two completely different systems, that of simple citations, and that of personal recasting. We wished to adopt the two systems by condensing, most of the time, the thought of the speakers and authors, without naming them, then by citing their own works. In the latter case the name is given, or reference is made to the volume by a Roman number, and to the page by an Arabic number. We have made explicit citations whenever we thought it opportune to emphasize a particularly interesting sentence, paragraph or page, or when we wished to leave to each author the responsibility and the merit of his rather delicate or very important affirmation.

Such a method has forced the editor to put something of his own into this work, because to condense into short syntheses the thought of several authors necessarily implies a choice; one must first assimilate the matter and then give it personal expression.

It is evident that this process does not substantially change the thought of each author or the burden of his message.

The material of our work is taken directly from volumes I and II (as far as page 523) of the *Acta et Documenta,* already cited. But in the course of the work the editor has chosen here and there among the other pages of volume II and of volumes III and IV, wherever the theme of the religious life is touched or treated, either incidentally or more or less extensively.

At the end of nearly all the thirteen chapters—in relation to their contents—the eminently authoritative and blessed words of Pope Pius XII are cited. We cite not only the pontifical documents published in the four volumes in question, but other sources also: "Exhortation to the clergy of the Catholic world" (Sept. 1950); (this is found only in part in the first volume of the "Acta et Documenta"); "Discourse to religious teachers" (Sept. 13, 1951) and the "Discourse to Superiors General" (Sept. 15, 1952); the encyclical letter "Sacra Virginitas" (March 25, 1954); the apostolic constitution "Sedes sapientiae" (May 30, 1956).

May God bless this work, undertaken for the sole purpose and with the sincere desire of doing good for many religious souls, and may it aid them to understand better and to live more perfectly the religious life.

May God grant us this grace through the maternal and powerful intercession of His mother, who is also ours.

FATHER VITUS GAIANI, O.F.M.

CHAPTER I

RELIGIOUS PERFECTION

1. THE IDEAL OF PERFECTION

It is of fundamental importance to have clear, precise and complete ideas concerning the ideal of religious perfection, an ideal which, like a lighthouse, must guide and draw the soul which is consecrated to such perfection.

What the Carmelite Father, Alexander of St. John of the Cross, writes concerning a good method of teaching novices is practical for all souls. Father Alexander writes: "Religious education ought not suppress the spontaneity of the novice, but rather lead and guide her. It should, moreover, awaken in her motives for her interior and exterior life. The novice ought not to have before her conscience a long, oppressive series of 'It is not allowed.' Rather she must feel in her conscience the command: 'Do not do it. Not because one is not allowed, but because, although you can do it, you will not, by reason of the ideal after which you strive.'

To keep the ideal always before one's eyes makes one love it. It seems to me that this is the chief duty of the master of novices and of every teacher." (III, 97)

The word *perfection* indicates a fulness, that is, the possession of all those elements that a thing or a person ought to have and the absence of those things that ought not to be had. Thus when we speak of religious perfection we wish to indicate the condition of a soul which does not commit voluntary sins and which strives to make progress in all the virtues.

Before treating of religious perfection, with the Dominican Father Cuervo (II, 338-345) we distinguish between spiritual perfection considered in itself, in relation to simple Christians, to religious, and to each soul in particular.

Spiritual perfection in itself comprises all the infused virtues and the gifts of the Holy Ghost in the fulness of their development, in as far as this is possible in the present life. Our Lord is the prototype of this perfection, and after Him His most holy Mother.

Regarding each Christian in particular one must distinguish between a perfection common to all the faithful, one common to all religious, that is, to those who live in the state of perfection, and a personal perfection proper to each of the faithful and to each religious.

The Christian perfection common to all the faithful consists in grace and charity which give us the possession of God, though imperfectly in this life, and the right to eternal happiness, making us attain the ultimate end to which we are destined.

The religious perfection common to all religious consists in the observance, not only of the commandments, but also of the evangelical counsels and of the obligations of one's state.

Personal perfection is the degree of sanctity which God expects from each soul according to the particular mission which Providence has assigned to each one and the degree of glory to which God has destined each.

2. THE ESSENCE OF PERFECTION—LOVE

The theological virtue of charity is the essence of Christian perfection. To love God in Himself, in us, and in our neighbor, to prove our love by doing God's holy will always and in all things, and thus to unite our soul with God, that is equivalent to living according to the ultimate purpose of our life which we will fully attain in heaven, namely the definite possession of God.

The theological virtues of faith and hope can co-exist with mortal sin: the other virtues do not attain God directly and immediately. Holy Scripture often recalls this truth to us. Jesus said in response to a teacher of the law: "Thou shalt love the Lord thy God. . . . That is the first and the greatest commandment. The second, which is similar to it, follows: Thou shalt love thy neighbor as thyself. On these two commandments the whole law and the prophets depend." (Mt. 22, 34-40) And St. Paul, faithful echo of his Master, affirms in a pithy formula: "The fulness of the law is love." (Rom. 13:10) Later Jesus stated precisely: "If you love me, keep my commandments." (Jo. 14:21)

Reason leads us to the same conclusion. In fact the goal of our soul is the love of a thing or of a person; knowledge is presupposed in order that one may love, for that which is not known cannot be loved, and the better one knows the value of an object, the more one loves it. Sincere love necessarily moves a person to do the will of the one loved; it moves from affection to action.

Seeing charity as the essential element in religious perfection corresponds perfectly to the modern soul's way of thinking and feeling. "It is impossible to doubt," remarked Father Melson, assistant general of the Carmelites, "that the actual physiognomy of perfect life is based on charity : . . . The perfection to which modern man tends does not stop at the graces or virtues, but at the person. Our desire is to go farther than the juridical fulfillment of the precepts. It is wearisome to calculate minutely how far one can go without sinning. He who loves, precisely because he loves, desires to give all. This holds also in that which concerns one's neighbor. Modern man is strongly moved to fraternal love. And if he sees it neglected he doubts the religious system itself. The chief element of life is placed in the object that one loves. Spontaneity moves more effectively as we see in the words of St. Augustine: 'Love, and do what you will.' " (II, 559)

3. THE LOVE THAT SAVES AND THE LOVE THAT PERFECTS

To the good young man who asks what he should do to attain eternal life Jesus answers: "If you wish to enter into life, keep the commandments." And when the young man answered that he had always kept them, Jesus looked upon him, loved him, and invited him to the love of perfection: "If you wish to be perfect, go, sell what you have and give it to the poor. . .then come and follow me." (Mt. 19:16-22)

The perfection proper to the simple Christian demands that he avoid sin, that he live and die in God's favor, in order to be assured of eternal salvation. The perfect Christian loves the Lord, obeying Him in all things that He has commanded. He observes, for example, conjugal chastity, respects the authority of the ecclesiastical hierarchy, and is not attached to the material goods that he possesses.

The perfection proper to the religious also demands that he love God in the highest possible degree in this life, also practicing the counsels of Jesus, which imply the voluntary renouncement of all material goods, of his own will and of marriage.

As the Dominican Father Llamera remarks: "Love is love's rival." The love of God can easily be smothered by the love of self, of the body, and of material things. That is why he who aspires to religious perfection renounces even lawful loves in order to make love triumph. (II:75-79)

The practice of the evangelical counsels (the subject will be treated explicitly later) removes the principal obstacles and breaks the strongest chains. Moreover it includes the exercise of many other Christian virtues, necessary for the right use of material things, of one's own body, of sense pleasures, of the will and of spiritual goods.

Thus the soul places itself on the shortest and easiest road for attaining the summit of virtue, the road pointed out by Jesus to the one who wishes to be perfect.

4. OTHER ASPECTS OF RELIGIOUS PERFECTION

Thus far we have emphasized the essential element of all spiritual perfection, namely, love. And under this aspect the religious life is an entire loving gift of the soul to God and to one's neighbor for the love of God. But love of perfection makes one attain marvelous goals which constitute other aspects of religious perfection.

It is a more perfect imitation of God made man, who lived in poverty, loving virginity, obeying Mary, Joseph, and His heavenly Father, even to the death of the cross.

To imitate Jesus as perfectly as possible has always been the great desire of the holy souls which are consecrated to Him. The invitation of the Master, *Follow Me*, finds a profound and lasting echo in their hearts, urging them to a constant and enlightened generosity in desires and in works, for their own sanctification, the glory of the heavenly Father, and the salvation of men.

Religious perfection is a more perfect union of the soul with Jesus and through Jesus with God. It implies greater conformity to Christ and more perfect divinization. But the soul of the simple faithful, in God's favor, is the branch united to Christ, the divine vine, participating in the life of Jesus and God. But a consecrated soul, faithful to its vocation, shares more abundantly in the life of Jesus and hence in the life of God. At a certain moment it can say with St. Paul: "It is Christ who lives in me." It is identified with Christ, within the limits possible, by its thoughts, its sentiments, its desires and its works.

The religious soul can also say: "I share in the life of the Holy Trinity, because I also know God and love God as God knows and loves himself, although not in the same degree."

"We are again made God-like," says the Jesuit Father Plus, "because we are Christianized." (II, 94)

Finally religious perfection is a greater prefiguration, imitation and anticipation of the life of heaven. For the consecrated soul the great difference between these two lives is the absence on earth of the beatific vision. Those who have totally consecrated themselves to Jesus, says Father Lombardi, S.J., have become "heavenly men. They have said good-bye to earth to become living witnesses of heaven." (I, 108) "We are on earth," says Father Plus, "a walking heaven; we have all that is essential in heaven except one thing, we do not see God." (II, 93)

"Tradition makes known to the religious that he has chosen an angelic life, that he sojourns in the midst of angels, according to expressions that go back to primitive monasticism. This foretaste of paradise is an invitation not to lose ourselves on the way." (I, 186)

5. BE PERFECT!

The one who follows Jesus by obeying the evangelical counsels has the obligation of striving after religious perfection. We say "of striving after perfection," not "of being perfect." A soul cannot become absolutely perfect on this earth. Jesus is such a perfect model that a soul will never fully reproduce Him in itself. God can bring it about that a soul know and love Him as He knows and loves Himself, but not in the same degree, otherwise such a one would be another God.

A comparison will help to clarify our statement. A pupil is obliged, not to know everything, but to learn all that is within his capabilities, which for various reasons will always be limited.

To tend towards perfection means to strive for it seriously, without pause or slackening of the will. It means making diligent use of all the means of perfection which are at our disposal. It means obeying with docility the divine Sanctifier of souls. That such an attitude is obligatory for a consecrated soul is beyond all discussion.

To every Christian soul is addressed the exhortation of Jesus: "Be perfect as your heavenly Father, who is in heaven, is perfect." (Mt. 5: 48) Every disciple of Christ ought to strive to resemble the heavenly Father and attain the degree of spiritual perfection which God expects of him.

But for a soul that is entirely given to God the goal to be attained is a greater sanctity in the spirit of the gospel, integrally accepted and lived. "If you wish to be perfect, go, sell what you have, give it to the poor. . . . Then come and follow me."

It is for this and nothing else that God has given to a soul the inestimable gift of a religious vocation. It is for this that the religious pronounces his holy vows, or makes other equivalent solemn acts, promise, oath, consecration, etc. It is for this that he lives in a spiritual greenhouse, as it were, rich in means well adapted to the end.

It is for this, above all, that he has been called to the Lord's vineyard, where he can carry on a fertile apostolate, but only if he is a soul totally given to God, ready for sacrifice, even heroic. "Only then," observes Father Llamera, O.P., "will it be connatural to him to sanctify others, as it is of the nature of fire to burn, of light to illuminate, of perfume to scent. Religious, sterile in themselves, cannot be fertile.

No one can be useful to others if he is not useful to himself. And this theology explains many of the sad religious stories, both individual and collective, for it indicates the reason why, although many labor for a work that demands a great deal of effort, the fruit is rare and disproportionate. Religious are not effective except as religious." (II, 81)

The Archbishop of Camerino, Most Rev. D'Avack, observes: "Today the laity, both the good and those less good, have more contact with religious. They perceive more easily the faults of religious, they take scandal from them more easily. . . . And . . . the demon . . . is busy enlarging these defects." (I, 295) "The laity in the world," says Father Lazzarini, editor of the Osservatore Romano, "love to feel near them. . . . These who are the living example of the Christian life. This example has more value for them than much preaching and discussion." (I, 294)

Again Archbishop D'Avack writes, "St. Benedict called for a profound interior work in the school of the Lord's service. St. Dominic wished to have contemplatives in order to make preachers out of them. St. Francis called for the unconditional imitation of Christ, poor and crucified. St. Ignatius proposed to his disciples the third degree of humility, humiliation. In spite, then, of all the inevitable human failings, do all religious really strive after these ideals? Or are these ideals considered as a souvenir of history, as coats of arms used by our ancestors and which we retain to decorate our hallways?" Archbishop D'Avack addresses the religious directly: "But if your positive acceptance of the demands of the state of perfection languishes—which God forbid!—what reason is there for your being in the Church?"

"Numerous, too numerous, are those who believe that Christianity is no longer capable of solving the terrible crisis of humanity. We know, thank God, we know and we believe that Christian doctrine is the only thing that can save humanity. But we also know that this doctrine can be summarized in two words: The first was pronounced at the moment of creation and of elevation to the supernatural order, the other was spoken by Christ for the restoration of humanity after original sin. These two words are *charity, cross.* We know that charity has been regained through the cross. And in order that the charity of the Head, Christ, should descend into all the members of His Mystical Body, this cross must be shared by His members. The more the cross of the Head extends to the members, the more grace realizes charity in men. Every action, every struggle against the enemies of God and of His church remains fruitless if the cross and charity are not lived more. It is very sad and disturbing that while so much zeal is spent fighting atheistic and anti-Christian communism and the communists, so much less effort is made to live the cross and charity. We may even say that the effort of too many Catholics, and not only among the laity, is to escape from the cross, from self-denial, from sacrifice. How many dissertations! How many subtleties! And that. . . is equivalent to denying Christianity in practice and opposing its divine power." (I, 299-302)

6. LIFE WITHOUT VITALITY

Such is the life of a consecrated soul which does not tend to perfection. Even if such a one gains salvation it will always remain true, sadly true, that he has not sanctified himself as he could and should have. And that will have been an irreparable pity for the soul itself, for the glory of God, and for the good of other souls. "A soul that saves itself," says Father Llamera, O.P. "is not a compensation for a soul which does not sanctify itself." (II, 88)

To the bitter disillusions are added the spiritual ruins. How many sins, more or less grave, follow as the fruit of laxity and lukewarmness! How many divine graces will no longer be given by Our Lord! How many scandals, always with bad effects, are given to other souls!

And what shall we say if the soul attains to formal contempt of religious perfection and of the obligation to strive for it? This would be a serious and odious fault, a prelude of probable reprobation.

But alas! "it is a fact only too well known," writes Father Cecchin of the Servites, "that many among us. . .are walking absurdities, in crying contrast between what we know or what we have to do, and what we are." (III, 154)

The life of a soul that is consecrated only in word is the life of an unfortunate misfit.

"The religious who is lukewarm," says Father Llamera, "lives for his misery and accumulates responsibilities. The advantages (of the religious) are changed (for him) into inconveniences, the privileges into miseries, the motives of perfection into sources of accusations. The yoke of religion becomes hard and its burden heavy. The vows which were bonds of love begin to be insupportable chains. The three characteristic advantages of the religious state, the vows thus change into so many hardships. These are so much the more burdensome because by the vows the religious

made a matter of obligation what was before superoga-
tory; he has made unlawful that which was lawful. Such
a life is the most false, absurd, and unhappy of lives, a life
without life, an apparent life, a dead life," because "only
the divine love which has caused it can sustain it: love is
the food, the strength, the life of this life." (II, 72, 75, 82s)

7. THE WORDS OF THE POPE

Let us listen to Pope Pius XII in his exhortation to the
clergy of the Catholic world September 23, 1950. "According to the teaching of our Divine Master, perfection of the
Christian life consists in love of God and of neighbor; love
which is truly fervent, eager, active. If it has these characteristics one can truly say that it embraces all the virtues
and can rightly be called the bond of perfection. (Col. 3:
14) In whatever state he may be, a man ought to direct
his intentions and actions towards this end."

In his discourse to the delegates of the International
Congress of the States of Perfection on December 8, 1950,
Pope Pius said: "There are those who say that the religious
state, by its nature and its end, which one must, of course,
approve, is nothing else than an anchor of salvation for the
timorous and restless, who, being incapable of sustaining
the struggle of a tumultuous life, not knowing how or not
wishing to face the difficulties, through pusillanimity abandon the world and take refuge in the peaceful harbor of
the convent. Is that true? It is not our task here to examine
the motives of each one who embraces the religious state.
We wish to show the principal and true reason for entering
the sacred inclosure of the religious life. It is far distant

from the theory that we have just mentioned, which, taken
in its generality, is false and unjust. Indeed the resolution
. . .to enter the religious state, and the firm decision to per-
severe in it, demands strong souls and an earnest desire of
immolation. The history of the Church, the illustrious
actions of the saints and of religious institutes, the success
of the missions, ascetic doctrines as well as experience show
clearly that in the religious state, no less than in the world,
there have been men and women of resplendent virtue.
However, the end that must always be kept before our
eyes—whether in the life of piety or in the apostolate—and
to which all the other children of the Church, priests and
laity, must tend, is Christian perfection and the salvation
of the human race. Now it is your duty to observe the
evangelical counsels, professed by the religious, as very
efficacious means in the assiduous struggle to subdue the
concupiscence of the flesh, the concupiscence of the eyes
and the pride of life; and thus to sanctify yourselves more
and to be untiring ministers of God in procuring the salvation of the human race." (IV, 315ss, 329s)

On May 30, 1956, in the Apostolic Constitution "Sedes
Sapientiae" Pope Pius wrote, "If the recommendation of
the apostle: 'Such is the will of God, your sanctification,'
holds for every Christian, how much more is he obligated
who . . . publicly professes the duty of acquiring evangelical
perfection, and by his own obligation is so constituted an
instrument of salvation for others that on his sanctity
depends to a great extent the salvation of souls and the
increase of the kingdom of God! Let all those who are in

the state of perfection recall the evangelical sanctity that they must acquire and let them meditate often before God that to fulfill the obligation of their profession it is not sufficient to avoid grave sins, or with the help of God, venial sins, nor to carry out in a material way the commands of superiors, (to observe) the vows, or the bonds obliging them in conscience, or their own constitution. It is indeed necessary that all this be accomplished with a wholehearted and fervent love, not only through constraint but through the duty of conscience; for to attain the summit in sanctity and to be living sources of Christian charity for all, religious ought to shine with an ardent charity for God and neighbor and be adorned with all the virtues." (AAS, XLVIII, 360)

CHAPTER II

THE STATE OF PERFECTION

1. STATE OF LIFE

When we speak of a young person choosing a state of life, we understand by this expression a stable and well defined condition of living, characterized by precise duties and rights, even with relation to the society which has given its approbation to the state of life. Thus we speak of the state of matrimony, of the priesthood, the religious state, etc.

He who passes from poverty to riches does not change his state of life, for both of these are unstable. Nor can we say that the fact alone of being in the service of another constitutes a state of slavery. On the other hand those who lived as slaves in the strict sense were in the state of slavery —and some still are, though the number is much smaller because of the progress of Christian civilization in the world.

From all we have said it is easy to see what the expression *state of perfection* implies: It indicates a stable condition of life, recognized and approved by the Church, in which the one who embraces it has the obligation of constantly striving after evangelical perfection, by making use of the means that this state offers.

2. STATE OF PERFECTION

He does not live in a state of perfection who, by his personal effort strives for perfection, binding himself by an obligation which holds only before God. The state of perfection implies a juridical, social aspect which, in the hypothesis, does not exist.

This juridical, social aspect is born of a juridical and social act, that is, of religious profession or of an equivalent act which incorporates an individual into a religious family, attaching him to it in a stable way, so that he contracts certain precise duties, acquires well defined rights, and is thus placed in a special category of the faithful, in a new state of life: in the religious state.

For the Church there are three juridical public states of life, the lay, the ecclesiastical, the religious. The first two—lay and ecclesiastic—have been willed by Our Lord Himself, who founded His Church as a hierarchical society, in which the apostles, their successors, and the others designated by them might be teachers and guides of all the other Christians, docile disciples and obedient members.

The religious state has been instituted by the Church for the purpose of controling, ruling and facilitating the means of tending to Christian perfection.

3. ORIGIN AND DEVELOPMENT OF THE STATES OF PERFECTION IN THE CATHOLIC CHURCH

In the first centuries of Christianity the souls called by God to evangelical perfection strove for it by their own effort while continuing to live in the world.

Thus there were the ascetics and the virgins, entirely consecrated to God by the private vow of perfect chastity, and often by the renouncement of material goods, and by various austerities. They even at times wore a special habit.

Already from the 3rd century other generous souls, imitating the life of St. John the Baptist, before his public preaching, and the example of Jesus, Who remained forty days in the desert, left the world materially and gave themselves entirely to the Lord in the eremitical life.

But the eremitical life entails dangers and does not offer the advantages of the common life, ruled in all details by obedience and lived by many souls equally desirous of striving for evangelical perfection. Thus other souls, especially enlightened by God, introduced various forms of the monastic life, founded colonies of monks (with prayers in common, etc.), monastic lauras (or villages with narrow lanes, surrounded by a hedge or a wall), and monasteries. And near the monks there lived also nuns, adapting to themselves the monastic way of life.

The time came when the Church, sole guardian and infallible interpreter of the holy gospel, believed it its duty to intervene by its supreme authority and in an official manner in an affair of such importance. The purpose of this intervention was to prevent possible deviations and to aid the holy intentions of so many privileged souls.

Thus it was, for example, that the Council of Chalcedon, in 541, established certain obligatory norms for the monasteries of men and women. They had to submit to the surveillance and direction of the bishops, observe the clausura, etc.

Even the Christian emperors of the fourth century were interested in this collective movement, in this new social class, whose progress they aided by favorable laws.

In this way striving after perfection on the part of so many souls consecrated to God was no longer a private affair, but took on a public, juridical character through the intervention of the Church in approving and regulating it. Thus was born the state of perfection, the ripe fruit of primitive asceticism. This state took different modalities, because with time, the changing ways of life, the multiple needs of society, God inspired and His Church approved other external ways of striving for evangelical perfection, each characterized by a spirit, an external form of the apostolate, an organization, a formation, a discipline of its own.

Thus it was that new congregations arose. For example the various families of the Canons Regular of the 11th and 13th centuries. These were secular priests who accepted the common life, a common rule, and embraced the evangelical counsels, to give themselves to the priestly ministry with greater surety and more abundant fruit.

Later the military orders were born, forming a holy militia, vowed to Christ, for the defense of the holy places and Christendom against the infidels. Likewise the orders of hospitallers and the mendicant orders, Franciscans, Dominicans, Carmelites, with their corresponding female congregations. Also the Clerks Regular, the Jesuits and the Camillians, etc; the societies of the common life, men and women, very numerous from the 16th century. Also the secular institutes, without public vows and without the common canonical life, recent sprouts of an admirable spiritual blossoming, fruit of a two thousand year evolution of the religious life, which has thus returned to its beginning.

Summarizing the history of the religious families of women, Cardinal Piazza said to the congress: "At the same time that the male branches flourished and continued to prosper, the families of consecrated virgins multiplied in an astounding way; from the first ones of apostolic times to the cloistered nuns. . . ; then came the Ursulines and the Visitation Sisters, who added some form of external activity to the contemplative life. Then in modern times the female congregations spread out in great number like flowers in the spring, so that today there does not exist in the Church a field of the apostolate where holy virgins, angels of goodness and purity, are not working and sacrificing themselves." (1, 97)

4. ACTUAL VARIETY OF THE STATES OF PERFECTION

Three classes of the states of perfection exist today in the church: religious or congregations in the strict sense; societies of the common life without public vows, and secular institutes without common canonical life and without public vows.

The elements which distinguish the one from the other are taken especially from the greater or lesser degree of recognition on the part of the Church and from the greater or lesser juridical and social effects of religious profession or its equivalent. (oath, promise, consecration, etc.)

The element common to all these states of perfection is the theological and ascetic: in each of them the soul must tend to evangelical perfection, conformable to the gospel, to the spirit of the religious institute and its specific goal.

Such an element is the most important of all. Father Gallone, superior general of the Company of St. Paul, a secular institute recently approved, thus describes the spiritual attitude of the first disciples of his religious society: "They ... did not even think of religious vows, not that they did not wish to give all to the Lord, but they seemed to see in them something of formalism. They aspired however to a full dedication to the Lord, to a formal engagement, consecrating their whole life to the apostolate. They made the solemn promise in a Eucharistic vigil like the ancient knights of the crusade. On coming to the community each one gave all that he possessed: money, activity, time, personal energy, asking nothing except to work for God." (2, 280)

We shall now mention some of the characteristics of the three actual classes of the state of perfection.

The religious or congregations in the strict sense incorporate their members by the profession of public vows, that is, of vows that are accepted by competent ecclesiastical or religious authority in the name of the Church. Such vows make the religious sacred persons, delegated to the public worship of God, having duties and rights that are not common to other religious persons; for example, the violation of these vows implies the particular malice of sacrilege.

Equal malice and guilt is imputed to any person who commits a real offense against a member of a religious order.

The societies of common life without public vows: Either there are no vows, or if there are, they remain private vows, though recognized by the Church. Indeed by means of indults and privileges they have often been placed on the same bases as the other congregations in regard to many things. They are a state of perfection, less solemn and, as it were, of second degree.

The secular institutes, finally, likewise recognized by the Church, have a legislation still milder than the societies, but not less sanctifying. Their members remain secular persons, subject to the canonical laws of seculars, whether lay or ecclesiastic.

Father Arcadius Larraona, secretary of the Sacred Congregation of Religious, says: "The secular institutes admit the consecration concerning in particular, but not exclusively, the counsel of perfect chastity. This consecration has been received, after examination, in the constitution 'Provida' as a possible form of gift to God and the Institute, provided it is not reduced to a vague ascetic formula, but that it be an offering clearly defined in its efforts and obliging in conscience before God and the Institute.

The Institutes may have vows, they may have the three ordinary vows—one only or several, provided that these particular vows are well defined, and, on the other hand, prove not only possible but also truly and surely useful, whether because of the particular goal of the perfection of the institute or because of its apostolate. The Institutes may also, in place of formal vows, make promises or oaths." (IV, 281ss)

Farther on, Father Larraona refers to certain papal documents from which the internal and external physiognomy of the Secular Institute is manifest: "They are clerical or lay societies whose members, in order to attain perfection and exercise fully the apostolate, practice the evangelical counsels in the world. . . . The whole life of the members of the secular institutes . . . ought to be changed into an apostolate which, with purity of intention, interior union with God, generous forgetfulness and abnegation of self, ought to be exercised in such a way that it manifests equally the interior spirit with which it is nourished and constantly feeds and renews this spirit." And he concludes: "The secular apostolate, ecclesiastic or lay, in the world . . . is considered compatible with the substantially complete life of perfection. Also the secular cleric, without ceasing to be such, can lead a life of perfection in a secular institute recognized by the Church. The laity also, raised to a higher rank, become not only collaborators of the hierarchical apostolate, as members of Catholic action, but they consecrate themselves to this apostolate by the perfect life which is intimately united with it." (IV, 292s)

Under the social juridical aspect, then, the congregations represent the canonical state of perfection in the strict sense; the societies of the common life, without public vows represent the state of assimilated perfection; and the secular institutes represent the state of perfection, which is not assimilated, although recognized, approved and ruled by the Church.

The legislation common to the congregations and societies is contained in the code of canon law, in the various responses given by the commission for the interpretation of the code and in the instructions, etc. of the Sacred Congregation of Religious. The common legislation of the secular institute is found especially in the apostolic constitution "Provida Mater Ecclesia" of 1947, in the Motu Proprio "Primo feliciter" of 1948 and the annexed instruction of the Sacred Congregation of Religious.

5. CAUSE OF THE VARIETY OF THE STATES OF PERFECTION

Religious congregations are numerous and there are also a good number of secular institutes. Very many associations of consecrated souls asked Mother Church that they be made secular institutes and some dozens among them have already obtained their desire. In Italy alone the congregations of women total 450. And the number of male and female religious in the world is around 1,200,000.

The intrinsic causes and the historical reasons for such a variety are various.

First of all, the ideal of evangelical perfection is so rich in themes, tones, and colors, that it lends itself very easily to a manifold realization by ways of life, identical as to substance, but differing by reason of the particular elements of each of them.

Hence the Church, the mystical spouse of Christ, in its admirable and truly supernatural fecundity, must give to God, besides innumerable adopted children, numerous families of consecrated souls, true choice flowers of the Lord in this earthly garden.

Father Mary Eugene of the Infant Jesus, O.C.D., makes an interesting remark on this point: "The creation of Catholic Action has associated the laity to the apostolic responsibilities of the hierarchy. The Institutes make the state of perfection fall into the ranks of the laity. The movements join to complete and perfect one another for the good of the Church and of souls." (II, 285)

To this same end Father Del Portillo, procurator general of the Opus Dei, secular institute recently approved, writes: "The members of the secular institutes being secular, love the seculars; and being totally given and consecrated to God, venerate and love the religious. Thus they tend to form a group half way between the two others, the religious and the faithful. The result is that, with the members of the secular institute, the army of the Church Militant appears more compact and completely harmonious." (II, 289)

Moreover, Divine Providence, with an infinite goodness and wisdom, acts in various ways at different times and places. It inspires founders and raises up, by means of them, choice groups of apostolic souls, who, by example, prayer, sacrifice, and various apostolic works, meet so many spiritual and material needs of human society. "As souls are different," writes Father Creusen, S. J., "as well as the graces they receive, so also are communities." (I, 477)

Another reason, finally, among so many others deserves emphasizing. The virtues and the works of Jesus have not been and cannot be imitated and accomplished fully by one or by several souls. Thus the Holy Spirit has inspired in different ways those who must become mother or father of a religious family. Now he draws one to the imitation of one virtue of the Savior, now of another, and moves souls to renew in the world here, that work of Christ, there, another, or this or that phase of the life of the divine bene-factor of humanity. For this reason the principal mysteries of the life of Christ, as also, in view of Him, the virtues and the life of the most Blessed Virgin, His mother, and of His foster father, St. Joseph, and the other saints, have found souls particularly devout, desirous of retracing them in their life.

Thus a Claretian Father, Martinez de Antonana, writes: "The life of Our Lord is living in His Church. . . ; and as it is the eternal object of worship and gives its variety to the liturgical year, it is fitting that it be as living and varied in the life of all His members, especially of those who are consecrated by vocation to His service." (I, 437)

6. ADVANTAGES OF THE RELIGIOUS LIFE

To avoid all misunderstanding let us at once say clearly that even outside the religious life a soul can, with the grace of God, attain the summit of religious perfection by practicing privately the evangelical counsels.

In fact the history of the Church tells us of saints who became such without joining a religious family. Thus they realized the ardent prayer of Jesus to the Father for the Apostles. "I pray not that thou shouldst take them out of the world but that thou shoudst keep them from evil. They are not of the world, as I also am not of the world. Sanctify them in truth. Thy word is truth. As thou hast sent me into the world, I also have sent them into the world." (John 17:15-19)

But it must also be said that the number of such saints represents a great minority among the total number of souls sanctified in the Church, because sanctity flourished especially in the closed gardens of religious families.

Among these latter, evangelical perfection is easier and surer because of so many efficacious means which the religious life offers to its members and the protections from dangers, which either are not found there or are very remote, or can easily be overcome.

Father Lombardi, S.J., puts it in these words: "Religious houses are true schools of perfection instituted by the Church. One could write at their entrance, 'Here sanctity is learned.'" (I, 113)

May every religious soul thank the Lord for having called him to the state of perfection—to an order, congregation, society or secular institute; let him love his state which is for him the best. And let him strive to make his own the numerous and precious advantages that it brings him in order to be able to attain more easily and more surely this spiritual perfection which God expects of him.

7. WORDS OF THE POPE

In his address on August 3, 1949, to the Missionaries of the Royalty of Our Lord Jesus Christ (pertaining to a secular institute), Pope Pius XII said: "Now that your virtue and your generosity have been recognized by the Church in a manner which has surpassed your expectations, it has ingrafted you into its life and has let you live in the world without being of the world. Is that not the wish that Jesus expressed regarding the apostles in His

High-priestly prayer? You are consecrated to God, recruited for the service of Christ; the pact has been sealed. God knows it, the Church knows it, you also know it. The world does not know it, but it feels the beneficent effects which radiate from the Christian substance of your being and of your apostolate. You are numerous and your vocation is to be the salt and the perfume of the earth, the leaven in the dough, the light of the world. You are in first place the leaven of the classes to which you belong by reason of birth, education and life, and from which you are not separated. You are also the leaven in the groups of friends where your activity and devotion is carried on. Finally, you are the leaven for that whole gathering of persons and of things where you fulfill your daily duties. . . However, your influence extends more vastly and profoundly into the apostolic fields, fertile and spacious, of Catholic Action. . . . You have lit this fire from the flame of the love of Christ which burned in the incomparable saint of Assisi. Thus we earnestly beg and exhort you, dear daughters, what the disciples of the seraphic patriarch did in the 13th century, do you now also, in very different circumstances but in the same spirit. . . . Open the hearts, make them capable of receiving the torrents of the love of Jesus. It is your role, Missionaries of the Royalty of Christ!" (I, 35s)

On the 21st of November in the apostolic constitution "Sponsa Christi," the Holy Father writes: "The Church, spouse of Christ from the beginning of its history, not only showed by frequent manifestations the sentiments of esteem and of maternal love with which it tenderly surrounds the virgins consecrated to the Lord, but it confirmed these sentiments in very important documents. This is not to be wondered at, because the Christian virgins, chosen part of the flock of Christ, urged on by the love of God, relinquishing the cares of the world, rise above the natural sharing of affections which is full of danger, not only to give themselves entirely to Christ, the true spouse of souls, but to consecrate their lives entirely, adorned with the precious stones of all virtues, to the perpetual service of Jesus and the Church. This mystical consecration of virgins to Christ and this devotion to the Church in the first centuries of Christianity developed spontaneously, more in facts than in words. When, afterwards, the virgins formed not only a class but a well-defined state and an Order recognized in the Church, the profession of virginity began to be made publicly and was strengthened by a still stronger bond. Afterwards the Church, accepting the holy vow or the resolution of virginity, consecrated the virgin as a person inviolably united to God and to the Church by a rite so solemn that it was rightly classed among the most beautiful of the ancient liturgy, and it clearly distinguished such virgins from the ones who offered themselves to God by private vows." (I, 73)

Finally on December 8, 1950, in an address to the delegates of the International Congress of Religious: "By the divine right itself it has been established that the clergy are distinct from the laity. Between these two great degrees is inserted the state of the religious life, which, of ecclesiastical origin, has its raison d'être and its value insofar as it adheres strictly to the proper goal of the Church which is to conduct men to sanctity. Although every Christian, under the leadership of the Church, must climb this summit, the religious ascends it by a way all his own and with the most sublime means. Moreover the religious state is not exclusively reserved to one or the other of the two categories which by divine right exist in the Church, for the clergy as well as the laity may equally be religious, just as the clerical dignity is available both to religious and to those who are not religious." (IV, 309s)

CHAPTER III

THE THREE EVANGELICAL COUNSELS

1. THREEFOLD RENOUNCEMENT IN VIEW OF A THREEFOLD CONQUEST

The practice of the three counsels, given by Jesus to the one who wants to be perfect, is the fundamental note of every state of perfection under the theological and ascetic aspect, even if it allows a very diversified scale of concrete applications which lessen or increase its severity, especially in regard to poverty.

In the intention of the Divine Master the three counsels of poverty, chastity, and voluntary obedience are destined to free the soul from three very serious obstacles which it meets in the way of perfection; obstacles caused by external goods, by the body tending to evil, and by the ego, struggling with self-love, attachment to one's own will and pride.

But this deliverance is not an end in itself. It is on the contrary a premise, a necessary preliminary condition in order that the soul may easily give itself entirely to God, loving Him in itself and in its neighbor.

"One must not," writes Father Larraona, "take the cross without the crucified, but one must take it with Him . . .

to find in Him resurrection and transformation into divine life." (IV, 299)

The vows or equivalent acts, common to every state of perfection, are not a renouncement for the sake of renouncement—that would be inhuman and absurd; but a renouncement of lesser goods for the conquest of higher goods; that is, the sovereign good, God.

"Our heart," writes Father Van Biervliet, C.S.S.R., "cannot remain empty. It necessarily fills itself with affections, earthly or heavenly. Everyone demands a good to which to give himself: an apparent good, which is the fruit of illusion, or a real good, God." (II, 56)

"The observance of the three counsels," remarks Father Llamera, O.P., "facilitates the perfection of divine love, because a perfect love is a unique love, entire and exclusive. The enemies of love are the human or temporal loves. And these loves, rivals of the love of God, are three in number, for there are three classes of goods that a man can love: external goods, bodily goods or satisfactions, and goods of the soul or will ... The evangelical counsels detach the heart from all that is created; they concentrate it on God. ... Free from every impediment, thanks to them, divine love absolutely dominates human life.

"Without the desire of perfect love these detachments would have no goal, these instruments would lack their effect." (II, 75s)

2. IS VICTORY POSSIBLE WITHOUT RENOUNCEMENT?

A soul can, absolutely speaking, attain Christian perfection even in the state of marriage, in the possession of material goods and with the free disposition of one's own will. The history of the Church does not lack saints who have lived thus, even on a royal throne. But this is not the ordinary thing. In their case there was perfect correspondence to the special graces of God.

It is indeed difficult—let us recall what Jesus said of riches—to enjoy certain natural goods without the heart attaching itself to them or using them in an inordinate way.

3. HARMONIOUS REALITY

Faithful practice of the evangelical counsels re-establishes in God's creature the original harmony, insofar as that is possible in this life. Material things serve man; the body serves the soul; and the soul serves the Lord. Thus all proceeds conformably to the end of the creation of things, of the body and soul.

Such a harmony enchants and attracts, whereas a mediocre spiritual life is without charm and taste for the one who lives thus as well as for the one who observes such a life. Only a religious life, intensely lived according to the double goal of the evangelical counsels—liberation and sublimation—and keeping the end to be attained always vibrating in one's heart and works, can become a powerful appeal for the souls desirous of giving themselves entirely to God.

Father Plé, O.P., gives a significant dialogue between a spiritual director and a young lady of 25 years, a social assistant, who without doubt had come to know, with a disagreeable surprise, religious who were not convinced and hence were not convincing.

"—When I read in the gospel the invitation of Our Lord, 'Come and follow me,' I have the impression that it is addressed to me.

—Which means no doubt, Miss, that you are thinking of entering the religious life.

—Oh never! I do not wish to be a good Sister.

—Why not? What have you against the good Sisters?

—They are too far from the gospel: They do not love one another; they do not pray but they recite prayers; they are not poor but economists; obedience dedicates them to infantilism; chastity makes them old girls." (II, 141)

CHAPTER IV

RELIGIOUS POVERTY

1. THE CONQUESTS OF EVANGELICAL POVERTY

Voluntary and real poverty is the most precise and explicit evangelical counsel. Jesus formulates it for the young rich man and repeats it again and again. "If you wish to be perfect, go, sell what you have and give it to the poor ... then come and follow me." Thus Our Lord puts poverty in direct relation with Christian perfection, which is the fulness of the love of God.

He who adheres with fervor to this counsel of the Redeemer does so because with equal faith and generosity he believes the other exhortations of Jesus: "Seek first the kingdom of God. ..."; "Store up treasures in heaven. ..."; "Be not solicitous as to what you eat. ..." Poverty is the riches of imperishable goods; a divine guarantee of the necessities of life as regards material goods.

If they truly live their promise, the voluntarily poor for the love of God become rich in goods even for their neighbor. Their way of living in common, without personal property, without waste of superfluous things and still less of useful things, without solicitude for tomorrow, without desire of commodities and amusements; such a life is a constant lesson for all those who in the world are eager and agitated for the possession and enjoyment of material goods.

Cardinal Siri writes on this point: "The actual social value of evangelical poverty appears to me to consist in this:

a) To show to men that, with true detachment of heart from material things, one overcomes all problems insofar as that can be done in this life. . . . The evils that worldly goods beget, whether in governments or in subjects, whether among the rich or the poor . . . proceeds from lack of detachment or liberty in regard to earthly things.

b) To show to men that, besides money, there are other goods capable of satisfying our existence, and in a way better than money. Existentialism has more partisans than communism, and most communists could consider themselves as existentialists, for they are for the most part malcontents, pessimists, accustomed to seeing what they do not have and failing to see what they do have.

c) To show to men that not only besides money, but besides all the good things that are called earthly, there are purely spiritual goods of greater value and much more capable of satisfying the life of man.

d) To show men that needs increase in proportion to human weakness, that one can live with very little . . . and that with very little one can not only live but can also be satisfied.

From what I have said it follows, with clear evidence, that the social value of religious poverty is realized only if it remains a true and complete poverty, in spirit and in practice. To be modern it ought to become an ever genuine poverty. . . . The world considers as being far from it those who are apparently neighbors; when it sees them near to it, it looks on them as itself (empty, vacant, and weak); that is, of little value. The world esteems those whom it sees stronger than itself. It considers stronger than itself those who are not slaves of its weakness." (I, 278s)

Moreover, the fact that the goods of the religious communities are ecclesiastical goods, administered according to canon law, necessary and useful for the mission of the Church on behalf of humanity, makes more apparent the sense of justice and of charity of the religious in the use of material goods, in conformity with the end that the creator has assigned to these goods, that is to say, the material and spiritual utility of all men.

For these reasons and others it is easily seen why the saints esteemed and praised so highly evangelical poverty.

2. NEED OF A GREATER REAL POVERTY IN THE STATES OF PERFECTION

Not all in the state of perfection practice poverty in the same measure.

In the most severe communities not only the simple religious but even the whole group renounces all ownership of material goods; they are content with a modest use of such goods. Ownership pertains to the Holy See.

In other communities it is a question of common ownership, not personal. In still others the ownership is personal but the individual cannot enjoy or dispose of his goods in any way without the permission of the superior, nor can he be the administrator of them. The so-called radical ownership is left to the individuals in order that they can more easily enter the state of perfection and more easily provide for their material needs in case they return to the world; in this eventuality they regain full possession of their goods.

But the criterion for judging the use of material goods in the spirit of poverty is not always the same. And this criterion would not be conformed to the Gospel if it permitted the use of these goods when superfluous or less useful or convenient.

From all sides and with ever greater insistence today one clamors for a greater poverty effective in the states of perfection.

"A poverty," says Father Lenzetti, O.P., "which does not limit itself to having to ask permission from the superior, but includes giving up superfluous things and even the useful and to accept in certain cases the privation of things necessary ... poverty, not only individual but social." (III, 113)

There are numerous motives for this. Let us recall some of them.

The real and extreme poverty of so many people in the world ought to recall all religious souls to a regime of life entirely in harmony with the promises made to the Lord and with the great sufferings of their neighbors. On the other hand it should incite them to a scrupulous observance of the norms of justice in that which concerns their lay employees, and as far as possible, to a generous liberality in favor of all the needy.

The founders of the various communities could not always prescribe, in all the external circumstances, what was certainly the most ardent wish of their heart for the good of their followers and for the efficacy of their apostolic works, that is, the most scrupulous fidelity to the example and teaching of Jesus who, as St. Paul reminds us (2 Cor.: 8), being rich became poor for us in order that we become rich, thanks to His poverty.

On this subject Bishop Ancel of Lyon, superior general of the Society of Priests of Prado, writes: "In order that poverty have its full meaning and its real efficacy for the sanctification of those who practice it, it is necessary . . . that it be an evangelical poverty, hence an effective poverty according to the example of Christ Jesus. No doubt dependence in the use of goods is necessary to avoid illusion; but the dependence essential to the vow of obedience ought to appear accessory, when it is a question of the vow of poverty. . . . The forms of poverty can vary but the reference to the poverty of Christ is a trait common to all the great religious families from their beginning. . . . Unfortunately, and under various pretexts, there is evident today a general diminution of evangelical poverty. There are, however, happy exceptions, whether in certain houses or even in entire societies. . . . The true spirit of poverty consists in depriving oneself effectively and as much as possible." (I, 380)

Father Middendorf, S.C.I., after having studied the poverty of Christ and of the Apostles in the light of the gospel accounts, concludes the first part of his interesting report in this way: "If anyone should say that there are as many ways of practicing poverty as there are religious institutes, after what we have just said, we would point out to him that it is just the opposite, for the imitation and the poverty of Christ during His public life are essentially one. Four essential qualities belong to every type of imitation of evangelical poverty:

1) For all who are called to the apostolate there is a common foundation: that they leave all, sell all, and give the price to the poor.

2) The common life is required in some way. It includes collaboration in activities under one head, having material goods in common, and a certain dwelling together. The common roof is not the substance of this life ... the common life in a wide sense as practiced in the secular institutes is fully conformed to the example of Christ and the Apostles.

3) Real personal and collective poverty ought to be manifest to the eyes of the faithful and of those whom it strives to convert. Otherwise these latter will not believe the ones who preach a kingdom of the next life.

4) Poverty is intimately bound to the preaching of the kingdom of God. Consequently, the apostolate must be addressed particularly to the poor. All religious are called to this apostolate. Pope Pius XII, on November 21, 1950, by the constitution 'Sponsa Christi' confided to all nuns an apostolate for the good of the universal Church by the example of a perfect life, by prayer and sacrifice, or by the works of charity and education. This holds, no doubt, for similar institutes; so that any community that is not apostolic does not exist in the Church.

Keeping these four basic elements, any institute or religious family can adapt itself to circumstances. A community which undertakes the education of children needs more money than one that applies itself to contemplation.

At the end of this chapter may we be permitted to present, as a conclusion of the preceding considerations, a fundamental request in practice, that is, that in all the religious institutes the faculty be given by law to the members to renounce spontaneously and freely all their goods for distribution to the poor."

3. PERSONAL OR COLLECTIVE DEFECTS IN REGARD TO POVERTY

Bishop Ancel writes: "Every relaxation in evangelical poverty is accompanied by an almost general relaxation of the whole religious life." (I, 380)

Such a relaxation is easy on the part of superiors and on the part of the community.

If one is constrained or authorized to handle money, the desire is quickly born of appropriating it to oneself, a desire experienced even by most prudent souls. "It is difficult," writes Father Maurus, O.F.M., Cap. of Grizzana, "to handle pitch and not to be soiled by it." (II, 176) And if one is not very careful, money is used independently of the superior. For example, when on a journey one may often presume permissions to buy things that are not really necessary.

If one has relatives, acquaintances, and friends, there will be occasions to give or to receive presents, which is often done without scruple.

The great St. Benedict in his holy rule thus anticipates this in his monks: "Above all let this vice be radically removed from the monastery so that no one dares to give or receive anything without the command of the Abbot, or have anything as his own. . . . The monks do not even have the free disposition of their body nor of their will." (I, 412)

And Pope Innocent III, in his decretal address to the Abbot of Subiaco in 1252 said: "Let not the Abbot dream of dispensing a monk in what concerns the ownership of goods; for the renouncement of ownership . . . is so bound up with the monastic rule that even the Sovereign Pontiff cannot make concessions in that matter." The Pope cannot dispense in such a way that the monk, remaining such, have something as his own, but the Holy Father can make of a monk a non-monk. (I, 420)

Has one the right to the use of many things? It is not difficult to use things with negligence and prodigality, forgetting that these things are not one's own but pertain to the Church and to the poor of Christ.

When the superior has given all that in conscience he thinks necessary and sufficient, there will always be some, who, forgetful of the state of perfection which is theirs and of the condition of life before their entrance into religion, will put forth demands beyond the normal. Already in his time St. Augustine wrote to the nuns: "Those who have goods in the world voluntarily accept that all be possessed in common. Let those who possess nothing not search in the monastery for those things which they would not be able to have outside. . . . And now let them not consider themselves fortunate because they have found the food and clothing that they could not have had in the world." (I, 411)

Finally, the spirit that one feels in certain communities is by no means stamped, as it ought to be, by complete detachment from earthly goods and by complete abandon to divine providence for the material needs of their members and of their works.

Sometimes one has the impression that an immoderate desire of gain seeks in earthly goods something else in addition to and different from simple instruments of spiritual good. Human prudence proper to the man of affairs in the world, consisting of calculations, budgets, and balance sheets, infiltrates into certain methods of administration. Let us hear the voices of particularly authorized men.

Bishop D'Avack writes: "During these last years one has seen a flowering of very beautiful religious houses ... edifices which are not strictly necessary nor urgent, at least not in their dimensions, beauty, and comfort, while at a short distance thousands of the faithful live in conditions that are very inhuman ... Is this the exercise of perfect charity? The people understand nothing of your distinctions: houses, provinces, the purpose. They take from this an awful scandal, and perhaps not wrongly. . . . So many religious founders again recently went to the aid of poor abandoned children, and now it is almost impossible for a child to be received without payment. It is true: the founders were saints and they worked miracles. But is it the chain of miracles that broke first, or that of sanctity? ... We see the works of great luxury from the clinic to the college; works which—it is easy to make the approximate cost—can never give such an income which would permit doing other gratuitous favors for the poor. Moreover, would not that be the more evangelical system? Works, then, which serve to help only the higher social classes are sought. All that would be very good, for they all have need, and what need! But, what is more, one helps them, not by educating them with delicacy and efficiency in the sense of sacrifice and of the cross of Christ, but rather confirming them in their privileges, their separation and their prejudices, thus putting them farther from Christianity." (I, 298s)

Mr. Borra, M.D., speaks of the sad reality in these words: "It seems that the great majority of active religious institutions were established to care for the poor, and that a great part of them have quickly passed to the service of the rich, predominantly, if not exclusively. Other institutions, which in their beginning were interested in the well-to-do nobles, remained in their help and in the service of the rich bourgeois, successors of the nobles. The common people, passing the foot of smiling hills on which sumptuous edifices are located, open only to well-provided burses, point to them as cultural, religious, and commercial institutions, incomprehensible at the present time, even if they have just been built. The more understanding and good Christians say, 'At least do a little charity; and, if you feel called (by whom?) to have colleges for certain privileged classes of society and hence endowed for you, leave a small place, a percentage of small places, gratuitous or with half tuition, for good students from the poorer classes. Of course, you are entrely free (if there is no pertinent civil law) to choose your students.' "

The well-known writer notes the other side of the picture, that of the ones concerned: "On their side they speak of enormous expenses to maintain a great number of members who are still in the process of formation . . . or who no longer earn anything because of age or infirmity. But the people see them waiting to buy ground, constructing veritable edifices and churches, even where there is a church close by. How can one picture an institution with self-respect that does not have its church? And, of course, this church must be worthy of the Lord and . . . of the Institution! These orders or institutes must be millionaires to spend money thus for themselves! There is a need for all institutions to develop; there are reasons of convenience; the necessity of reasonable and beautiful constructions; there is an external appearance which ought to be in proportion to the social importance of the institution, etc. Men experienced in business reply that the industries, banks, etc., say the same thing, or nearly the same; they construct luxurious buildings for service or representation. The new institutes, as is human, present different aspects of the crisis of growth; they need to develop their bones, they concentrate all their energies in new constructions and in the ever vaster organization. They say: just now we cannot concern ourselves with the poor; but indirectly—or directly, according to the point of view—we are also doing good. The more ancient institutes emphasize the need to modernize. Deep in their hearts they admit they could dispense more charity. And if they are asked, they make it part of their plans for the future. But the good people think: will they be in time? Sumptuous colleges, elegant convents, villas, theatres, cinemas, speculations, etc., hurt the poor people. Is the production of moral good really bound to the elegance of the edifices? Is there a direct relation between the splendor of the constructions and the moral influence of these holy institutions?"

Finally, in regard to costly vacations for religious, Dr. Borra observes: "Everyone realizes the necessity of good health, the need for many intellectuals to interrupt their work of the mind. But the people ask: Is it possible that certain religious are so sick, for example, with liver trouble, and in such a great number, that they must construct a villa purposely in a famous hydrothermal center, where during the summer they arrive with faces that show no sign of liver illness? The poor worker who is not able to take a vacation thinks that it is not indispensable to spend a month in the mountains in summer, then a month at the sea and again a month in the country! Is the poverty of the religious purely juridical or real?" (I, 310, 314)

Finally, Cardinal Siri notes: "It seems to me opportune to consider the problem of the poverty not only of persons, but also of institutions. Not that they may not possess anything (save certain particular constitutions), but there should be certain restraints, for one has the opinion that with many there is too much political economy, to the peril of confidence in providence and of that kind of life which authorizes us to put more hope in providence . . ."(II, 21)

The servant of God, Canon Joseph Allamano, founder of Consolata Missionaries, who in the course of forty years collected and dispensed seven million dollars, regulated his conduct on principles that he announced as follows: "If it is necessary to spend something, we should not consider how much money is had, but how great is the necessity in relation to the divine will. If the expense is necessary, it is to be made even if the money is not at hand; the Lord will provide. . . . The expenses which I have to make for the institute do not disturb me, though they are always increasing. What disturbs me is not whether the money will come, but whether we shall merit that it come. If we merit it, the Lord will make it come and go; otherwise, it will only go. . . . When man mixes himself in the matter, God withdraws." (I, 651) As to the solution, St. Don Bosco laments: "It is not possible for me to find a procurator who will back me up entirely, who knows how to confide in Providence and does not seek to make provision for the future. I fear that if one find himself pinched for finances it is because one wishes to do too much calculating." And speaking to his confreres of the divine chastisements inflicted on the communities forgetful of evangelical poverty, object of their religious vows, he commented in these words: "On the ruins of these Orders are born new congregations. Jesus has been generous to them and will be so again if they are not attached to riches." (I, 651s)

Father Giampetro, S.J., in a volume written for religious, rightly says: "We consecrated souls, we are by profession witnesses of the gospel teachings and we must act with greater coherence, for example, in that which concerns poverty, which we solemnly profess before God and men. It is true that in each Order or congregation there is a way (approved by the Church) of practicing this virtue, and each one observes it holily, but there are facts and things which are unbecoming in any religious."

The conclusion of Father Gallea, I.M.C., is very interesting: "The spirit of poverty is great capital and sufficient by itself to maintain all the religious of the world. Where it flourishes it makes plentiful the means which they need for themselves and for their works, and leaves no room for the superfluous. Then the tasks of collecting funds is no longer destined to enrich, or for more comfortable living, but to aid one's neighbor; the care to be sparing is not avarice but an exercise of detachment for the things of the earth. The solicitude of the procurator is not anxiety for tomorrow, but the competency of the good and faithful servant whom the Lord has placed over His house in order that he supply what is necessary to his servants." (I, 652)

4. WORDS OF THE POPE

On November 25, 1948, speaking to the Capuchins, Pope Pius XII said: "Having renewed, or rather reawakened the spirit and the breath of your institute, you wish to undertake new enterprises, adapted to modern conditions and the needs of the times. What is more desirable than such designs, what is more salutary than such works? The union of new and ancient things is demanded by the law of life itself in order that life be always the same and constantly at work. For this reason the form of religious life that you have been destined from your beginning to cultivate and establish ought to be observed with care in its entirety. That which, without doubt, your glorious fathers have proposed to themselves and to their confreres, even of the future, and which ought to be safeguarded with the greatest zeal, is to cultivate evangelical poverty according to the commandment and example of the patriarch of Assisi. What a deluge of evils is due to the detestable thirst for riches: from that come wars, seditions, famine, decadence of morals, ruin! The great difference between those who are too rich and those who languish in misery and hunger cause mortal wounds. The example of evangelical poverty is an admirable remedy for this calamity and corruption; it is the companion of the holy activity commanded by God, it is the friend of virtues, the teacher of peoples, the support and honor of the reign of Christ, the faithful depository of a better hope. Its noble standard has been confided to your hands: keep it without spot. It is not becoming to profess it with affectation and in fallacious terms, and then, indeed, trample upon it with one's feet." (I, 31)

On September 23, 1950, in his exhortation to the Catholic clergy (all that is said to the ecclesiastics applies still more to religious, to whom the Pope alludes incidentally): "To detachment from your will and from yourselves by generous obedience to your superiors, and to renouncement of earthly pleasures by chastity, you must add detachment from riches and from worldly things. We ardently exhort you, dear brothers, not to attach your hearts to earthly goods. Take as your model the great saints of the past and of the present who, uniting the necessary detachment from earthly goods to a very great confidence in Divine Providence and to an ardent sacerdotal zeal, have accomplished admirable works, trusting only in God, who never allows us to want for what is necessary. The priest himself, who does not make profession of poverty by a special vow, must be guided by the spirit and love of this virtue; love that he ought to show by the simplicity and modesty of his life, of his house, and by his generosity to the poor. In a very special way let him detest mixing in enterprises of an economic order that would impede the accomplishment of his duties of shepherd and lessen the consideration of the faithful. The priest, before applying himself with all his heart to the salvation of souls, ought always be able with St. Paul to say of himself: 'I do not seek your goods but yourselves. . . .' Your zeal must have as its object, not earthly and perishable things, but those which are eternal. The goal of the priests who aspire to sanctity must be the following: to work only for the glory of God and the salvation of souls. How many priests, even in the present serious conditions, have had as a norm the examples and advice of the Apostle of the Gentiles, who was satisfied with the indispensable minimum. 'Having food and sufficient clothing, with these let us be content.' (I Tim. 6,8) This most praiseworthy disinterestedness and detachment from earthly things, united to confidence in Divine Providence, has permitted the priestly ministry to give to the Church abundant fruits for its spiritual and social well-being."

On December 8, 1950, speaking to the delegates of the International Congress of Religious, Pope Pius said: "Recently we have informed the faithful, that in these unfortunate times, when distress and lamentable poverty contrast sharply with the luxury of others, they should live modestly and show themselves generous towards their neighbor who is oppressed with poverty. Indeed, by your example lead the way for others in such an important work of Christian perfection, of justice and of charity, and lead them to the imitation of Christ." (IV, 331)

CHAPTER V

RELIGIOUS OBEDIENCE

1. THE CONQUEST OF RELIGIOUS OBEDIENCE

Here everything can be summarized in one fundamental affirmation: religious obedience takes away from the one who obeys the practical possibility of abusing his liberty by making him do the will of God always in all things with constant denial of self, which is highly meritorious.

The world is infuriated in a special way against this vow of obedience. The world calls it a slavery, a cruel destruction of human personality. According to the world it would be better if every soul were completely free from itself, for thus only can it do many excellent things, better than those that are ordered by others, exploiting in full its qualities, its natural inclinations and acquired aptitudes.

But it is clear that the world, speaking in that way, shows that it understands nothing of religious obedience.

Indeed, far from destroying personality, true obedience, made of real natural and supernatural values, elevates and enobles one to the highest level, making the individual truly great, rich and happy.

It is religious obedience which frees the individual from the most powerful obstacle in the way of the good: the possibility of using his will to do evil. How many failures in individuals, families and societies, were caused by license, by instinctive resistance to every commandment, by the mania for independence in regard to everything and every person!

Father De Libero, of the Oratory at Rome, writes: "From Kant to our day the poison of autonomy, in regard to God and men, and stupid self-rule in politics brought the revolution to us, the revolution which is very popular today under all forms and in all social strata. Of course the meaning of liberty has been lost and to be free today means to do what one wants, even to kill if that is what one wants to do." (II, 416)

It is religious obedience which makes the one who obeys accomplish that which is best in the eyes of the Lord, and hence also for himself. What difference does it make to the obedient one if he sometimes has to sacrifice his natural inclination in part or entirely, or some acquired ability, when he is sure of doing the will of God in his regard?

He is certain at every instant of seconding the movement of the Holy Spirit, the divine sanctifier of souls. He makes his own the special grace that God gives to superiors that they can guide the children of God in the ways of the Lord. He lives in peace.

Precious and wonderful fruits of religious obedience are this security, this richness, this peace! "When a religious," writes Father De Libero, "has become quite poor in everything, he no longer finds a reason or force whatever which can make him half-hearted in the accomplishment of an obedience, much less determine him to go contrary to the will of his superior. He is like a train without resistance in its gears, without resistance on the way, and which advances gently, without injury and without jolts. The one who obeys becomes a rich man well on the way towards his end, rich in interior and exterior liberty; rich in peace, who finds in himself, as it were, the promise of the reward he will receive hereafter. Safeguarded and made subject, nature is sustained by grace which, as a gentle and propitious wind, swells and pushes the sails of our ship on the stormy sea of life enroute towards eternity. This sublime obedience has its perfect model in Jesus, who knew how to immolate even His physiological needs such as hunger.... 'My meat is to do the will of Him who sent Me....' His obedience culminates in the words pronounced during the agony in the garden: 'My Father, not as I will, but as Thou willest.' The Church, in the course of the three days of the week which is well named holy, seems to have no more beautiful eulogy for Jesus before the Father than the following: 'Christ made Himself for us obedient unto death; unto the death of the cross.'" (II, 217s)

If the value of obedience is so great for souls in particular, its efficacy is no less great for their social apostolate. Only obedience saves them from numerous dangers and makes them choose the most apt means for the salvation of their neighbor. And only obedience makes compact the army of the sons of God in the struggle against the demon and his strongly organized and very clever supporters.

2. THE TRUE AND UNIQUE FOUNDATION OF RELIGIOUS OBEDIENCE

The religious obeys because he knows that he who commands (the superior ordinarily) has the right to command, insofar as he holds the place of God and commands within the limit of his authority.

The superior, in a fuller sense, and above those who are such in the community, is the Pope, the Sacred Congregation of Religious, the Bishop of the diocese (in the matter recognized by the laws of the Church). It can be also any person delegated by the responsible superior of a given branch of activity.

De Libero writes: "We obey Christ in obeying the superior, as when on earth He gave an order to one apostle, then to another. . . . As the authority of the supreme commander of the army descends, always more limited, divided and subdivided in the generals of various grades, the colonels, etc., as far as the corporals, it is always to this very last, the unique authority of the supreme commander; like the electric energy from a central station, whether it feeds large lamps or small ones, it is always one and the same energy. Thus in the Catholic Church, the ecclesiastical authority, no matter whence or in what way it comes, it is always the authority of its head, Jesus Christ." (II, 414)

Today the cult of personality is fashionable, and in its name one can be tempted to consider less the authority of the one who commands in the name of the Lord and the legitimacy of his orders than their solid foundation, their reasonable aspect.

Today it is the democratic spirit that is honored. And even a religious soul can deceive himself and pretend that between him and the superior there are, so to say, democratic relations, that is to say, relations of trust and, as it were, of equality, where the subject, while recognizing himself as such, should prefer to be a collaborator, to whom all personal initiative is allowed, and who has the right to consider the motives of the orders given.

In particular cases the superior could give the reason for certain commands, for example, to new religious who have grown up that way, or to the young, not yet well trained and little inclined to obedience. But if this had to be done in all cases religious obedience would lose its supernatural aureola of free, conscious, unconditional, and filial adherence to the will of God, manifested by His representatives. There would be no more place for the exercise of the other virtues, such as faith, renouncement, humility, etc. And religious obedience would be reduced to a lay, external obedience without merit, based only, or in a predominant way, on the principles of natural character; on the necessity of a hierarchy, of rule or discipline in any human society; or on the qualities of the one who commands.

3. EXTENT OF RELIGIOUS OBEDIENCE

The religious who is seriously striving for perfection obeys his superiors not only when they command in virtue of holy obedience or its equivalent, but also when they express any order, desire, or counsel.

An ancient controversy remains unsolved today on the obligatory character of particular laws of every state of perfection, which are designated under the name of rule, constitution, etc. The question is this: "Does he who transgresses such rules commit sin or is he merely at fault in regard to purely directive norms, and in conscience must he only submit to the punishment provided for by the laws?"

The question has never been defined in a general way by the Church. And the various states of perfection, with a few exceptions, in practice adopt this principle suggested by the norms—No. 320—promulgated by the Holy See in 1901: "Of themselves constitutions do not oblige in conscience and hence the one who disobeys them does not sin, except when he transgresses through contempt, or in matter which concerns the observance of the vows, of the commandments of God, or of the Church."

The recently deceased Father Muzzarelli, who had been procurator general of the Society of St. Paul and consultor of the Sacred Congregation of Religious, wrote: "Let it always be permissible to affirm that this principle is often badly interpreted, in such a way that many, in the practical application, are really led into error. . . . It seems that the principle that the constitutions do not bind, ought to be enunciated in a different way, more appropriately, more completely, and corresponding better to the actual concept of the constitutions (not an appendix to the rule, of secondary value, but a unique code, often of the particular legislation of a congregation). We reach this conclusion if the non-obligatory character of the constitutions is enunciated in the following or equivalent fashion:

1) The rules that relate to divine or ecclesiastical laws retain the obligation that they have of themselves.

2) The rules which concern the vows, that is, which tend to determine the remote or proximate matter of the vows, receive this obligatory character from the vows themselves.

3) The prescriptions which regard government and define its necessary functions, the burdens and the offices that it implies, likewise those things which fix and consecrate the nature and the specific end of the congregation, oblige in conscience, according to the gravity of the matter.

4) The purely disciplinary or ascetic prescriptions, not comprised in the preceeding, do not oblige, of themselves, under pain of sin. They oblige directly and in conscience that one accept the punishment for their violation, and no doubt they may constitute matter of the vow and of the virtue of obedience.

Moreover it is a fault to violate any rule, even the least, out of contempt.

If one transgresses for a reason or purpose that is not right, for example, through laziness, through lack of necessary mortification, through an inordinate habit, or for any other bad reason; or if the fault gives scandal or contributes to laxity of the religious life: in all these cases the transgression implies a sin against the corresponding virtue." (I, 540)

Other authors suggest important considerations: a) Whoever is striving for perfection must not neglect the explicit wishes of the Lord which form a code of sanctity, in harmony with the spirit proper to each congregation.

b) The particular laws of every state of perfection are not merely counsel, but a concrete indication of what is better, coming from legitimate superiors who have made them and from the Church which has examined them attentively and at length; they have been tried out in practice and finally approved.

c) In Canon 593 the Church simply affirms that "all religious ought to live according to the rules and consitutions of their community."

d) Finally there can be the danger of understanding religious obedience by subtle reasoning on the vow and the virtue of obedience, on the laws that bind only as to punishment and those that imply a guilt. The result of all this is to reduce the matter of obedience to a minimum.

Concerning this matter the Carmelite, Father Anastasius of the Holy Rosary, writes: "It seems that an excessive legalism has, in fact, minimized the fundamental function of obedience, especially when considered as a vow. The distinction between vow and virtue has rendered almost non-existent the actual exercise of the vow in the habitual life of the religious and has rendered problematic even the matter of the virtue with the doctrine of laws which bind only 'ad poenam' and not 'ad culpam'. Thus one may believe that a re-evaluation of obedience from the dogmatic and ascetic point of view, would be a true and salutary renewal, which would aid especially in a juridical elucidation of obedience. To this end the value of consecration by vow, the connection of obedience with faith, with the supernatural state of the perfect life, are the most determining aspects for transforming religious obedience from social exigency to a personal life of perfection, that is, of charity." (II, 408)

And Father Lenzetti, O.P., says; "There are many books on the vows but not all are equally recommendable, because several, less clear and theological, insist too much —that is the least one can say—on the distinction between vow and virtue. I hope that the religious life remains attached to its true traditions, without rejecting all that is modern. It is one thing to legislate in the matter of the vows and religious life; it is something else to live this life. The viewpoint of the ascetic and of the jurist differs. In formulating laws and commentaries let us maintain the positions of an authentic theology of the religious state. . . . The vow of obedience is the one that suffers most abuse from the distinction between virtue and vow. If one restricts the obligation to the formal command, how can one maintain that obedience is the basic vow, the first for victory over self, which is the principal obstacle to the triumph of charity?" (III, 112s)

Father Gambari, of the Montfort Fathers, pointedly observes: "All admit the obligation in conscience of undergoing the penalty inflicted for transgression. But is such an obligation sufficient force and sanction for those who are engaged in striving after perfection? Many constitutions do not have a prescribed penalty. It seems more opportune ... to establish a certain obligation in conscience as belonging to every precept and prescription of the rules and constitutions. . . . One might ask if it is useful to insist on the obligatory character of the articles of the rules and constitutions—safeguarding, however, the opportune distinction between the articles which contain prescriptions and those which are only exhortations—by establishing the obligation in conscience, even under the pain of sin, for the more important prescription . . . ; and that, in virtue of the constitutions themselves, without need to recur to other reasons. Practically one must say that the statement, 'The constitutions do not oblige under pain of sin,' has nearly no concrete application. Indeed, even when one abstracts from the culpable motive of the transgression and makes exception for the ascetic and purely disciplinary articles, nearly all the others imply an obligation in conscience, even under pain of sin. . . . In fact, then, what are the other articles in the constitutions that do not oblige in conscience?" (I, 526s)

4. BLIND AND DEAF AND DUMB OBEDIENCE

The saints and other spiritual writers have vied with one another in defining and describing in many ways the qualities of religious obedience.

Let us consider some examples. The rule of St. Benedict seeks a prompt, cheerful and humble obedience. St. Ignatius of Loyola establishes three degrees of obedience, to obey by the spirit, by the will, and by the carrying out of the command.

The Capuchin Father, Maurus de Grizzana, commenting on the invocation of the Our Father, "Thy will be done on earth as it is in heaven," writes: "One wishes to indicate the perfect union of our will with that of God; union which is complete and perfect in heaven between God and the blessed. . . . There is no intention of identifying the two wills, but to force the human will to walk parallel to that of God. The comparison of the railroad tracks which run along endlessly without deviating even a millimeter, to assure the running of the train, tells us something of what the will of man ought to be in relation to the will of God." (II, 420)

A word of explanation must be added concerning another formula, very commonly used, demanding a blind, deaf, and dumb obedience.

The same Father Maurus of Grizzana explains it thus: "Blind, he who sees nothing else but God; deaf, he who gives no attention except to the voice of God; dumb, he who discusses the commands of God." (II, 421)

Religious obedience is blind and it is not blind. It is blind in this sense, that it is not based on the fact that the commandments of superiors or of laws are more or less reasonable. It is not blind in the sense that it presupposes and affirms that superiors are legitimate, and that their laws or commands conform to the general and particular goal of every state of perfection, and do not require heroic acts—which cannot and ought not be demanded of all—nor ridiculous or useless acts.

And in a wider sense, the subject, in obeying, makes use of an intelligent sense of initiative and of responsibility. He must, in fact, penetrate the spirit of the laws and commands of the superiors and apply them to unforeseen cases, not restricting himself to the purely material, formalistic obedience of a robot. There are circumstances in which one is excused from literal obedience to the law and commands. On other occasions one may claim exemption, having recourse to *epikeia*, supposing that the legislators or superiors in such a case, would, if they were present, give a dispensation.

Religious obedience is deaf and dumb and it is not deaf and dumb. It is deaf and dumb in this sense that it does not admit a reply to the legitimate and final command of the legitimate superior with personal restrictions of "if" and "but." It is not deaf and dumb because it permits the subject to humbly manifest to the immediate or higher superior his difficulties and his point of view, on conditon, well understood, that he adhere to the final decision of the superior without wishing to impose his own will.

5. BEWARE OF DIFFICULTIES

Obedience is a great and beautiful virtue, but it is very easy for religious to be imperfect in this matter. Let us note a few of the more frequent violations.

He does not obey who pushes himself ahead by trickery or by an interested servilism, instead of showing indifference in regard to the type of work and to place of residence.

He obeys himself and not his superiors who speaks and acts in such a way that the superiors finally change their decision to satisfy him.

He is lacking in obedience and in the other virtues who murmurs to himself—or, still worse, in the presence of others, criticizes—the orders of his superiors, he who internally resists their commands, even if he obeys them; who goes so far as to discredit the very person of his superiors.

He is not seeking the will of God who excuses his disobediences by pointing his finger at the faults of the superiors. The superiors, of course, are not impeccable or infallible.

The superiors may make mistakes; that is their affair before God. The subject ought to obey even if he doubts the opportuneness of the order of the superiors.

On the other hand the one obeying ought to be on guard concerning the too human sentiments which certain good and bad superiors can give birth to. That is not supernatural, religious obedience which is based on sympathy or on affection; in such a case one obeys rather the human person than the representative of God.

6. THE DUTY OF SUPERIORS

Superiors, commanding in the name of Our Lord, ought to imitate, in their governing, the qualities and virtues of the divine government.

The Very Rev. John Baptist Janssens, superior general of the Society of Jesus, recalls the necessity of imitating, above all else, divine wisdom, striving to examine things carefully before deciding, even asking the advice of the one whom we know does not agree with us.

The superior ought to imitate the constancy of our Creator, not changing his decision which has been taken after mature deliberation, unless new reasons come to light that have not been considered before.

"But, above all," adds the Very Rev. Father, "the superior, whether in the things he commands or in the manner in which he does it, will strive to imitate the incomparable delicacy of divine charity. He will command with humility, with tact and measure, putting himself in place of his subjects and demanding from them only things that are reasonable, moderate, and normally possible.

The subjects are not tools or machines: they are human beings, endowed by the Creator, in different degrees, with qualities of intellect and heart, and provided by the divine liberality with gifts of initiative, which vary from the little initiative of a capable cook to the vast initiative of a founder. It enters into the plans of divine providence that all these riches, which God distributes among creatures return a hundred-fold or as much as possible. A superior who would try to smother under the pretext of dependence, all initiative in his subjects, would merit the reproach made by Our Divine Master to the servant who buried the talent entrusted to him. On the contrary, it is the highest art of superiors to utilize to the greatest measure humanly possible, all the resources of their subjects."

The Church has never admitted that all initiative must come from above; the approbation and decision, yes; the proposals, the experiences, the beginnings, no. To cite only a few known and evident examples: The institution of the feasts of Corpus Christi and of the Sacred Heart; the Marian congregations, the work of the propagation of the faith, the Apostolate of Prayer, the Legion of Mary are so many institutions begun by those subject to authority, and afterwards approved and consecrated by those in authority.

Therefore let the superiors seek to harmonize authority with the initiative of their subjects, leaving to them a fitting sphere of action.

7. WORDS OF THE POPE

September 17, 1946, in a discourse addressed to the Jesuits, Pope Pius XII said: "In order that our wish be happily realized you must observe certain conditions. First of all you must be entirely faithful to your constitutions and to all their prescriptions ... Let obedience be your passport, your pride, your assurance; let this virtue make you entirely pliant, without wicked criticisms—the disease of our time—which dissipate our powers and render apostolic enterprises languid and inefficacious. The burdens imposed by an austere obedience will make you docile to the breath of charity which assures us of the presence of God, for God is charity." (I, 21s)

On December 8, 1950, in a discourse addressed to the delegates of the International Congress of Religious, Pope Pius XII said: "If the number of those—especially among young girls—who wish to enter into the closed garden of the religious life, diminishes, most often it is because they fear too much to be deprived of free will and to renounce their liberty, a thing which the very nature of the vow of obedience demands. And certain ones exalt as a sublime form of moral perfection, not the renouncement of liberty for love of Christ, but the greatest possible lessening of this renouncement. According to them, in forming men to justice and sanctity one ought to prefer the following rule: Let one restrain liberty as much as is necessary, let one leave the bridle free as much as possible! We are not stopping here to examine the question whether this new foundation on which one strives to construct the edifice of sanctity will be equally promising and solid for upholding and developing the apostolic work of the Church, as that which for 1500 years has consisted in the ancient rule of obedience, embraced out of love for Christ. What is extremely important at this moment is to consider thoroughly such a theory so that what is hidden may be clearly manifested. If one examines it attentively one must say that it by no means recognizes the nature of the evangelical counsels, it even overturns and corrupts it to a certain extent. No one is obliged to impose on himself the observance of the evangelical counsel of perfect obedience who has as a basis this norm of life which demands the renouncement of the free use of one's own will; no one, we repeat, is obliged to do this, neither individuals nor groups of men.

If they wish, they may order their life according to the above-mentioned rule. But the words must be taken and received in their true sense. Now if one compares this norm with the vow of obedience, it certainly does not have so great a value, it does not reproduce the doctrine and example of scripture, 'He humiliated Himself, becoming obedient unto death.' (Phil. 2:8)

Thus the one who gives counsel about entering the religious life, and who proposes to follow only this norm or theory, neglecting the inclination of the soul and the movement of the grace of God, is deceiving himself. Thus, if the invitation of the divine voice by signs that are sure, calls someone to the heights of evangelical perfection, putting aside all hesitation for the purpose of realizing this sublime aim, let one intend the free immolation of his liberty demanded by the vow of obedience, by the vow, we say, that the Church throughout the centuries has always esteemed, defined and approved. Let no one be forced against his will to make this sacrifice, but if he wishes it, let no one dissuade him from it, much less, hinder him." (IV, 317-320)

On May 30, 1956, in the apostolic constitution "Sedes Sapientiae," Pope Pius XII wrote: "Let all those striving to attain perfection remember and frequently consider before God that, in order to accomplish the duties of their profession, it is not sufficient for them to fulfill only in a material way the commandments of superiors or to observe in the same way the vows or bonds obliging in conscience, or the constitutions, according to which—conformably to the laws of the Church in the holy canons—each and every religious must order his life and thus strive for the perfection of his state. Indeed, all these things must be accomplished with all one's soul and with an ardent love, not only through constraint (to avoid chastisement), but also because conscience so dictates, for in order to climb the summits of sanctity and to show themselves for all, living sources of charity, they must burn with a charity inflamed for God and neighbor and be adorned with all virtues." (AAS, 360)

CHAPTER VI

RELIGIOUS CHASTITY

1. ITS NOBLE CONQUESTS

To be only and always the faithful spouse of Christ and to have perfect love for Him and one's neighbor, to become mother of many souls—this is the noble goal that a soul purposes to attain in promising to God perfect and perpetual chastity in a state of perfection; this is the better part, says Jesus, which is not understood by all but only by the privileged whom the Lord enlightens. (Mt. 19:10s)

This is the way one must understand and live religious chastity if one wishes that renunciation be justified, that perfect practice become possible and even easy, that all its fruits be ineffably sweet.

Having cited these principles, let us listen to illustrations of them given by fervent priestly souls.

The diocesan priest, Livius Labor, penetrates and develops these ideas in such a persuasive and convincing manner that he merits to be cited here at length.

"All Christianity is summarized in the love of God for His own sake and love of neighbor for God's sake. To strive for evangelical perfection is to strive for the perfection of love.

The excellence of chastity does not consist merely in the renouncement of marriage but also in the renouncement . . . of conjugal love, in order to tend immediately to the perfection of love of God, with the totality of His being, and to the perfection of love of neighbor with a great liberty and apostolic universality.

Perfect chastity has its adequate reason and its entire explanation in the theological virtue of charity, from which it proceeds, by which it is fed, and to which it returns.

This reality ought to be clearly and efficaciously presented, so that . . . chastity gives the effect of a joyful victory, even if it is necessarily conditioned by an indispensable renouncement—and a renouncement not of an evil, but of a good for a higher good.

Perfect chastity thus tends to a more direct, total, immediate consecration of the whole man to God, and not only under the spiritual aspect (higher faculties), but also under the psycho-physical-sensible aspects, insofar as it endeavors to spiritualize them and to transform them little by little to a supernatural tendency.

The life of apostolic chastity is rooted in the tendency to the greatest union of holy nuptials with God . . . and in the tendency to apostolic paternity and maternity towards the souls in particular and towards the human communities, the families of other groups and social sectors.

All the inspiration, the richness, the capacity, the strength, the gift, the abandon, the generosity of conjugal love, divinized by the renouncement of human marriage and of the sensible joys of love, are not lessened, nor impoverished, nor made sterile, but are elevated and enriched by perfect chastity.

Thus one establishes a relation of love with God which from purification to illumination and to union ascends towards its love, love which will be consummated in eternity. . . .

In such a perspective apostolic chastity appears not as an expedient against the nature of man . . ., not as an amputation, a snuffing out of the capacity to love, but an elevation, and the greatest pouring out of the power of the human creature to love; which . . . transports into Christ and, with Christ into the apostolic family, all the possibilities of natural love—rendered supernatural by charity—and does not know barriers to apostolic love for souls without number."

"To avoid regrets, understandable nostalgias, psychologic loss of balance, and even sad and tragic mistakes," adds Abbé Labor, "it is absolutely necessary to understand and to envisage apostolic chastity 'in all its real and incomparable theological and social light.' Thus it is necessary to avoid 'the ephemeral and abusive grandiloquence which can excite artificial enthusiasms due to sudden and brief phases of religious exaltation.'" (II, 313s)

On this point Father Maurus de Grizzana, O.F.M., Cap., writes: "In the natural exigencies of life it is not sufficient to introduce renouncement of paternity or maternity. The negative side alone could signify a form of egoism. The positive side has greater importance.

If the soul cannot always have something better than the attraction of the flesh, something higher to attract and satisfy it, renouncement does not imply a sufficient justification, and remains a pure violation of nature, depriving it of legitimate satisfactions.

On the other hand in the providential order of God no one can withdraw himself from the duty of producing . . . . To beget a body is a beautiful thing, but to beget souls, and in an unlimited number, is something still more beautiful and wholly divine; the one peoples the earth with citizens, the other peoples heaven with elect.

Chastity, understood in the light of such a mission, is certainly possible and secure. If human love is renounced completely, God's love will possess one's heart. And in such a state there is no more danger to chastity. The religious may well find himself in contact with any human shamefulness whatsoever and with all that could entice the flesh: there will be nothing to fear. He will have the occasion of becoming more firm in his resolution, appreciating it better in comparison with human miseries. In these contacts, while he witnesses the most bitter disillusions of life he will see that his aspirations to the contrary are never disappointed, whether in the gift of self to God or in devotion to souls.

Although we must not neglect the necessary precautions for chastity . . . the first and indispensible defense must be organized at an opportune time in the order of ideas . . . destined to become life and life in action. It is necessary that the religious be able to look at all the earthly joys, not with the regret of one who has made a useless renouncement, but serenely and with the joy of one who has found something better, not only in ideal but in practical life, and of which he already tastes the fruits." (II, 179s)

2. OTHER RAYS AND PERFUMES OF THE WHITE LILY OF RELIGIOUS CHASTITY

Chastity relates the religious to the angels because, like them, he consents to live a life totally consecrated to his ultimate supernatural end; while married persons are plunged, even in a permissible and holy way, into earthly preoccupation and human affections. The fully chaste religious soul is like the sanctuary lamp, like the flowers placed on the altar of God.

Religious chastity is more precious than virginity preserved intact by many souls in the world, because it is irrevocable in the intention, thanks to a solemn promise, because it is recognized juridically by the Church and is kept not only for its own sake, but also and especially in view of evangelical perfection and the religious apostolate.

One can say that it has a greater value than religious poverty and obedience. For these virtues leave something to the one who professes them: poverty leaves the use of necessary and useful things; obedience often commands things which correspond fully to the way of living and the tastes of the one who obeys. But chastity takes all, and urges the renunciation of every sensible affection which approaches imperfection and lack of mortification.

3. INDISPENSIBLE PRECAUTIONS

Religious chastity is a treasure contained in a fragile vase; it is a mirror which is easily soiled. All that we are to say later about religious mortification applies especially to purity.

Of this Father Fiocchi, S.J., writes: "Regarding chastity we must demand that the rules of precaution be more and more inculcated: every Institute has its own rules which are approved by the Holy See. But it often happens that they are eluded under divers excuses, especially in the parlors and the hospital services." (II, 163)

Father Maurus de Grizzana, O.F.M. Capuchin, says: "Besides fidelity to the keeping of the vow of chastity, one should also look for new safeguards or strengthen the old ones in face of new perils. . . . The walls of the cloisters were a protecting hedge. . . . Now for many religious things go otherwise, they not only rub elbows with persons of the world, but they are engaged . . . in studies and works that put them in direct and immediate contact with that which can be a true, not an imaginary, danger for chastity. Very characteristic is the work in hospitals and also, in part, missionary work." (II, 179)

4. RELIGIOUS CHASTITY AND FRATERNAL CHARITY

The religious, in giving himself to God and his neighbor, for love of God, gives himself above all—after God—to his closest neighbor, the religious family of which he is a part.

Thus there is established an atmosphere of mutual benevolence, of anticipating goodness, of holy sympathy, and of supernatural affection, of reciprocal service and relief.

"In whatever place the brethren find themselves or meet," writes St. Francis of Assisi in the 6th chapter of his rule, "let them show themselves familiar and manifest with confidence their needs to one another. For if a mother nourishes and loves her son according to the flesh, it is with a much greater affection that each one ought to love and nourish his spiritual brother." (I, 182)

Such a manner of living with other members of the community permits the heart to pour itself out supernaturally, fully corresponding to the natural inclination of man who is by nature sociable.

Where perfect chastity finds the authentic breath of Christian charity and the holy fervor of religious fraternity, there will disappear, as by magic, all the forms of intransigent rigorism, of proud insensibility, of cold inhumanity, rightly denounced and condemned by many.

Father Jambart, S.J., deplores that community life where there is no fraternal union, which is nothing more than "the life of travelers who do not know one another and whom chance has united in a hotel for some hours." (II, 27s)

Let us recall the severe denunciation of St. Francis de Sales: "We desire to be good angels in such a way that we cease to be virtuous persons." More recently Dom Columba Marmion wrote: "Let us stop being pharisees; otherwise, while willing to be monks one can come so far as not to be Christian, nor human, failing in the natural precept of charity." (I, 182)

In a study prepared in the supplement of ALA (October, 1955, p. 33ss) Father Joseph Giampetro, S.J., denounces among ascetical errors also angelism, "that tendency to wish to consider the human being a spirit, neglecting to take into account that he is also a body, even that he is a rational animal."

Let us summarize here some of the numerous observations he makes.

To insist on the duty to live with angelic manners, to recommend imitation of the purity of the angels may be a praiseworthy exhortation, but to avoid all equivocation let these things be well explained, for we must do good according to our nature. "Even the most perfect practice of charity does not take away from us our sentiments and our sensibility."

Note the fine precision offered by Father Massabki, O.S.B.: "The orientation of the heart from conjugal and maternal love to more spiritual ends is made by degrees and not without difficulty. Watching over the heart does not imply the suppression of all natural and supernatural friendship: such a suppression could cause one to become unbalanced. . . . Even human love of one's neighbor is still love of God. Impurity does not consist in the presence of the flesh but in the domination of the flesh over the spirit. When it stays in its place the flesh exercises an important duty. . . . The real masters of the spiritual life are not ignorant of this need of the human heart."

Abbot Marmion writes: "The angels must love God without heart, sentiments, affection. . . . But God wishes that man love Him in a human way, that is, with all his heart, with all his soul, with all his strength, and with all his spirit, and his neighbor in the same way. It would be unbearable if we were obliged to act like souls without bodies. . . . Let us not continue to make too much of the sublime; let us be content to act with simplicity; and let us ask to love Jesus with detachment, in such a way that no human affection may become necessary. . . . Use affections like you use other creatures: do not stop at creatures if you desire to use them according to the will of God."

The frequent distinction of religious into two classes merits particular mention. It is necessary to take care that such a distinction does not strike a blow at fraternal charity. "Recent inquiries," writes Father Plé, "have revealed that certain congregations have a mind to simply suppress the lay brothers and sisters; and that others, more numerous, strive to lessen the differences." (II, 144)

Father Marschal, C.SS.R., writes: "Every community forms an organic unity, as one mystical body, which has its head and its members; but whose work is one, coming from all, and as such agreeable to God. From one end to the other of its social being . . . it is a communion of saints; it is the very mystery of the Church in miniature. The sense of this compenetration, of this oneness of life must characterize the life of all its members."

"It is evident," he continues, "that the number of lay brothers grows smaller and smaller. An inquiry was made in France among sixty-nine orders and congregations to discover the cause of this penury. And it has been recognized that the principal cause is the lessening of fraternal union between the two classes in the communities. Hence one sees here again that the principal remedy would be to intensify this life of union, a solution which each institution will realize in its own way, in line with its spirit and traditions. . . . The lay member himself, who has made himself a helper, is conscious that his role is subordinate to the service of the common good. He is not opposed to it. Subordination is too much a part of the state of human affairs to be contrasted with the dignity, the legitimate professional sentiment, which the worker today so highly prizes. This subordination is found elevated in its spirit by the precious advantages that it discovers in this union of life and action. But the disillusion would be too hard if, from the life of union, of fraternal charity, of esteem and of comprehension, there remained for the worker only the dependence of the laborer whom one commands, the inferiority of the servant, permanent subjection to heavy and tedious work, distributed without discernment, without any mark of sympathy. Never to have anything to say, never to be consulted for the tasks at which he is competent . . . is to ask heroism of the lay (Brother) religious. We are far from the beautiful Franciscan characteristic: 'Brothers first of all, the distinction of priests and lay religious takes second place.' The lay brothers are not to serve the community, nor are they destined to the apostolate; they are members of the family in an atmosphere of fraternity. We return to the axiom revealed by the inquiry in question: The more a religious family leads a life of union, the more lay brothers it has. . . ." (III, 197ss)

Father Donnarumma, O.F.M., thus concludes his brief report: "I earnestly exhort all religious not to see in lay religious coadjutors or servants. Let them not be considered as inferiors but as equals since they are children of the same mother and make profession according to the same rule to attain a noble ideal. How often the crisis of vocations of lay religious is due to this factor!" (III, 221)

Father Rosa, S.J., writes: "I do not see the necessity nor the fitness that there exist different classes among the lay communities; whereas, it is opportune or even necessary in clerical communities. Among these latter, however, it seems to me, that the diversity of classes should not extend to a social viewpoint. Under this aspect there should be but one class only, since the members of these communities are children of the same mother, the congregation. If then, on the one hand, the lay members owe a particular respect to those who are priests, on the other hand they will be treated as brothers." Regarding the shortage of vocations of lay brothers he gives this reason: "The different treatment and the little esteem that is given them. . . . That makes the community undeserving of other vocations." (III, 222ss)

If in religious families—truly such—chastity would always bloom and flourish in a sincere fraternal love, how much suffering, how many secret tears, and how many defections would be avoided!

5. WORDS OF THE POPE

In a letter to the Prior General of the Hospitalers of St. John of God, May 20, 1947, Pope Pius XII, wrote: "In the present times religious are more exposed to the danger of losing their vocation or of becoming lax, because of the circumstances, of the infirm of all kinds, and of those for whom they must care, with whom they must be in contact to give assistance or direction. If then they are not well founded on very solid virtues, if they are not moved entirely by a high esteem of the duty of their office, they will with difficulty resist the attractions of the world, and in less favorable times, its menaces." (I, 25)

On September 13, 1951, addressing religious teachers, Pope Pius XII, said: "Chastity, virginity, which implies also the interior renouncement of all sensual affection, does not make souls strangers to the world. Rather it awakens and develops energies for greater and more sublime works which go beyond particular families. There are today numerous religious teachers and nurses who are, in the best sense of the word, closer to life than the ordinary persons of the world."

Speaking to the Mothers General on September 15, 1952, the Holy Father said, "Be mindful that the vows have demanded from your sisters as from yourselves a great sacrifice. They have renounced their family, the happiness of marriage, the intimacy of a home! This is a sacrifice of great value, of decisive importance for the apostolate of the Church, but always sacrifice.

Those of your sisters whose souls are most noble and most delicate, feel this detachment profoundly. The word of Christ: 'He who, having put his hand to the plow, looks back, is not fit for the kingdom of God' finds its entire application here, and that without exception. But the Order must take the place of the family as far as that is possible; and you superiors general are called in first place to put into the common life of sisters the warmth of family affections."

Let us again cite at length the precious encyclical letter, entirely consecrated to Holy Virginity. (March 25, 1954)

Father Arcadius Larraona, secretary of the Sacred Congregation of Religious, writes in regard to this encyclical in the presentation that he makes in the review ALA (June, 1954): "The Holy Father, happily reigning, will always be recognized by history as a valiant defender of the religious life in modern times. The proof of this is the numerous discourses given during various audiences to members of religious institutes, the wonderful congresses held in various nations, the luminous directions, the constitution, *Provida Mater,* which inserts in the religious system a new form of life, and the encyclical, *Sponsa Christi,* which answers needs of cloistered sisters of our epoch. And behold now this new and very opportune gift. . . . The 'Sacra Virginitas' teaches us that spiritual love is not negative. The soul that consecrates its virginity to God does not deny human love; it does not destroy it but elevates it. And it elevates it to the extent that it extends it. Purely human love, if it is intense, limits and concentrates itself. Virginal love, the more it is developed, the more it extends itself. It is never limited: all have an abundant share in it." (141s)

Hence let us pick out from this admirable letter the principal passages, which we shall divide into three sections.

A. *Nature and Excellence of Virginity and of Perfect Chastity*

"Holy Virginity and this perfect chastity which is consecrated to the service of God, is, without doubt, one of the most precious treasures that its Founder has left as a heritage to the society He has established, the Church.

Perpetual virginity is a superior gift, of essentially Christian origin. . . . If the pagans of antiquity demanded of the Vestal virgins such a type of life, they did not impose it except for a time; and when in the Old Testament the keeping and practicing of virginity was prescribed, it was ordained only as a preliminary condition for marriage. . . . Since apostolic times this virtue developed and flourished in the garden of the Church. The multitude of the faithful who, since the beginning of the Church, have consecrated their chastity to God, is incalculable, some keeping their virginity intact, others vowing their widowhood to Him at the death of their spouse; others, finally, have chosen a chaste life after having done penance for their sins.

Virginity cannot be a Christian virtue if we do not embrace it 'for the kingdom of heaven,' that is, if we do not accept this condition of life in order to be able to apply ourselves more easily to divine things; to be more certain one day to attain eternal beatitude; to be able, finally, to lead others more freely to the kingdom of heaven.

Those Christians, therefore, cannot claim the honor of virginity who renounce marriage through selfishness or to avoid its responsibilities, or even, after the manner of the pharisees, to proudly parade their bodily integrity.

The holy fathers have considered this bond of perfect chastity as a kind of spiritual marriage by which the soul unites itself with Christ. . . . The writings of the doctor of Milan, St. Ambrose, attest already in the fourth century the great resemblance between the rite of the consecration of virgins and that of the nuptial blessing still in use today. Moreover, the holy fathers exhort the virgins to love their Divine Spouse more than they would love their own husband and always to conform their thoughts and actions to His will.

If, finally, all those who, in one way or another, are vowed to the service of God, observe perfect chastity, it is because their Divine Master was a virgin even till the end of His life. 'It is indeed the only Son of God,' writes Saint Fulgentius, 'only Son likewise of the Virgin, only Spouse of all holy Virgins, fruit, ornament, and recompense of holy virginity, Him whom holy virginity has begotten, whom it espouses spiritually, Him through whom it becomes fruitful without lesion to its integrity, Him with whom it is ornamented to remain beautiful, Him whom it crowns that it may reign eternally.'

But if we consider the abundance of fruits which come from it, then without doubt, its excellence is shown forth more clearly for 'One knows the tree by its fruits.' We cannot but feel a great and sweet joy at the thought of this numberless phalanx of virgins and apostles who, from the beginning of the Church to our time, have renounced marriage to consecrate themselves more easily and more completely to the salvation of their neighbor through love for Christ, and have used such admirable initiatives on the plane of religion and charity.

Those indeed follow and direct the life of men of every age and condition, of a generous heart; and when they succumb to fatigue or infirmity, they confide to others the continuation of their sacred mission as a heritage. Thus it often happens that an infant is hardly born before he is gathered in virginal arms, and that nothing is wanting to him that the mother herself could have given with her intense love; likewise when he has grown up and has reached the use of reason he is entrusted to those who can give to his soul the teaching of Christian doctrine, fill his mind with profitable sciences and form his faculties and his character in the right way. If someone suffers from a sickness or is afflicted with other evils, he is surrounded by those who, animated by the charity of Christ, strive to restore him to health by their vigilant care and fitting remedies.

The orphan and the prisoner do not want for comfort and aid. Priest, religious, holy virgins will see in him a suffering member of the Mystical Body of Jesus. . . . What shall we say to praise the heralds of the word of God who, far from their country, bear the most oppressive labors to convert multitudes of infidels to the Christian faith? What shall we say of the holy spouses of Christ who give them the help of their very precious collaboration?

Virginity is fruitful, not only through the initiatives and the external works to which all those who embrace it can devote themselves more easily and more completely, but also by reason of the forms perfect charity can take in regard to one's neighbor, as are their ardent prayers for his intention and the great privations supported spontaneously and voluntarily for the same reason. For all that the servants of God and the spouses of Jesus Christ—especially those who pass their life within the cloister—have consecrated their life.

Finally, virginity consecrated to Christ is a testimony by itself of such faith in the kingdom of God, shows such love of the divine Redeemer, that it is not to be wondered at that it produces abundant fruits of sanctity. For these virgins and all those who give themselves to the apostolate and vow themselves to perfect chastity, by the great sanctity of their life are, in an almost incalculable number, the honor of the Church. Indeed this virginity gives to souls such spiritual strength that it can, if necessary, lead them even to martyrdom.

It is not without reason that virginity is called the angelic virtue. St. Cyprian, writing to virgins, says: 'What we shall be later, you begin to be already. By persevering in chastity and virginity you are equal to the angels of God.'

To the soul thirsting for pure life and burning with the desire to reach the kingdom of God virginity is offered 'as a precious stone' for which a man 'sold all that he had and bought it.'

As to those who are married, and even in regard to those who wallow in the mire of vice, when they see virgins, they often admire the splendor of their purity and they feel urged to the pursuit of that which must surpass the pleasures of the senses. . . .

Virgins manifest and make public the perfect virginity of their mother the Church and the sanctity of its close union with Christ. For virgins the greatest glory is that they are the living image of this perfect integrity which unites the church with its divine Spouse.

They offer, moreover, an admirable fertility by which the society founded by Jesus Christ excels and procures to this same society an immense joy.

That is why St. Cyprian writes appropriately: 'It is the flower that opens in the Church, the honor and ornament of the spiritual beauty, the joy of its nature, a work of praise and glory, perfect and without blemish, the image of God corresponding to the sanctity of Our Lord, the most illustrious part of the flock of Christ. The Church rejoices over it, she whose fecundity flourishes abundantly in these souls; and the more the multitude of virgins increases in number, the more the joy of this mother increases.'

B. *Errors Concerning Virginity and Perfect Chastity*

Those who consider the natural sexual instinct as the most important and the greatest inclination of the human organism and consequently conclude that one cannot, during his whole life, restrain such an instinct without incurring the grave danger of injuring his body and especially his nerves, and hence of doing harm to the equilibrium of his personality, are without doubt in error. . . . It pertains to the directing impulse of human reason, this singular privilege of our nature, to rule the impulses and instincts and to ennoble them and to direct them with righteousness. . . . But the grace of Christ is given to us especially by the sacraments, in order that, living by the spirit we may reduce our body to servitude. The virtue of chastity does not demand of us that we do not feel the prick of concupiscence, but rather that we subject it to right reason and to the law of grace, to make it tend with all our strength towards that which is most noble in human life. . . . The soul will be able to reign completely over the body and to lead a tranquil and free spiritual life.

Recently we have, with regret, condemned the opinion of those who go so far as to say that only marriage can insure to human personality natural development and desired perfection, . . . that it is a more efficacious instrument than virginity to unite souls to God, because Christian marriage is a sacrament whereas virginity is not. We denounce in this doctrine a dangerous error. . . . The sacrament (of matrimony) was not instituted as some kind of a most suitable means in itself to unite the souls of the spouses to God by the bonds of charity.

Finally, one cannot affirm, as certain ones do, that the 'mutual aid' that the spouses seek in marriage, is, for their sanctification a more perfect aid than—according to their expression—the solitude of heart of virgins and of those not married. Indeed the souls consecrated to perfect chastity do not impoverish their human personality, for they receive from God Himself a spiritual help immensely more efficacious than the mutual aid of the spouses. . . . They do not impoverish but rather enrich themselves.

Some discourage young people from entering seminaries and religious institutes under the pretext that the Church today has greater need of the aid and example of Christian life from those who are united in marriage and live in the midst of other men, than of priests and religious who because of their vow of chastity, live separated from human society. Such an opinion is as false and dangerous as can be. It is rightly in virtue of perfect chastity, embraced by them, that these priests and religious can give themselves entirely to all men and love them with the love of Christ Himself. And even those who give themselves to the contemplative life certainly contribute much to the welfare of the church by their fervent prayers and the offering of their immolation for the salvation of their neighbor. They are even greatly to be praised, for in the actual circumstances they consecrate themselves to works of charity according to the rules given by Us in the apostolic letter 'Sponsa Christi.'

C. *Means of Observing Virginity and Perfect Chastity*

Virginity is a difficult virtue. . . . For many, indeed, perpetual continence would be a burden much too heavy to be recommended to them. . . . Its faithful and perfect practice is possible to souls who, after a serious examination, correspond with a generous heart and do all in their power to practice it. Indeed by embracing the state of virginity or celibacy they will receive from God a grace sufficient to maintain their promise. That is why, if there are souls who do not think that they have received the gift of chastity (even if they have made the vow) let them not pretend because of that not to be able to satisfy their obligations on this point, because 'God does not command the impossible, but in commanding He counsels to do what you can and to ask for that which you cannot do, and He helps you to succeed.' Let us recall this truth, consoling also to those whose will has been weakened by nervous troubles and to whom certain doctors, sometimes even Catholic doctors, too easily advise—under the fallacious pretext that one can never preserve chastity without harming their mental equilibrium—to free themselves from their obligations. How much more useful and opportune it would be to help these sick to strengthen their will and to convince them that chastity is not impossible even for them, according to the Apostle's word: 'God is faithful and will not permit you to be tempted beyond your strength, but with the temptation will also give you a way out that you may be able to bear it.' (I Cor. 10:13)

The means recommended by the divine Redeemer Himself to efficaciously preserve our virtue are constant vigilance and prayer. For this reason we must above all watch over the movements of the passions and the senses. We must master them by voluntary austerity of life and bodily penances. . . . If someone, by reason of bad health or for other causes, cannot practice bodily austerities, this must not dispense him in any case from vigilance and interior mortification.

In this matter it must be remembered . . . that it is easier to overcome the allurements of sin and the attractions of the passions by avoiding them through prompt flight than by attacking them directly. . . . Such a flight consists not only in carefully remaining at a distance from the occasions of sin, but above all, in raising our spirit during the struggle towards Him to whom we have consecrated our virginity. . . .

However, it seems that not all think this way today. Some hold that all Christians . . . must be present in the world and therefore it is necessary to try them and to expose their chastity to trial that they may show whether they have the strength to resist. . . . But it is easy to understand how erroneous and dangerous this method of education is. . . . What gardener exposes young exotic plants to inclemencies under pretext of experience?

Educators will . . . perform a much more praiseworthy and useful work by inculcating the laws of Christian modesty.

This virtue anticipates the peril which threatens, prevents one from exposing himself to danger, and counsels one to avoid the occasions to which the less prudent expose themselves. It does not like unbecoming and vulgar words, and it has a horror even for slightly immodest behavior; it makes one avoid suspicious familiarity with persons of the other sex. Such a soul has a horror for every sin of impurity and steps aside immediately every time it feels itself attracted by its seductions. Modesty moreover suggests to parents and to educators the appropriate terms to form the conscience of the young in regard to purity.

It is nourished by the fear of God, this filial fear, based on a profound Christian humility, which makes us hold in horror the least sin. . . .

To keep chastity perfect and without spot and to make it grow stronger there exists a remarkable means which has not ceased to prove its worth throughout the centuries. It is a solid and fervent devotion to the virgin Mother of God. In a certain sense all the other means are found contained in this devotion. He who is animated with it sincerely and profoundly is, without doubt, urged to watch attentively, to pray, and to approach the tribunal of penance and the holy table with fruit. That is why we exhort, with a paternal heart, all priests and religious to put themselves under the special protection of the Mother of God, who is the virgin of virgins, 'the teacher of virginity,' according to the expression of St. Ambrose, and who is especially the powerful mother of all those who are consecrated to the service of God . . . confide to Mary the care of your spiritual life, imitating the example of St. Jerome who said: 'For me virginity is a consecration to Mary and to Christ.' "

CHAPTER VII

THE VIRTUES IN THE RELIGIOUS LIFE

1. THE THEOLOGICAL VIRTUES

The three theological virtues of faith, hope, and charity are supernatural faculties of the soul, which in baptism, through sanctifying grace, is made an adopted child of God and a sharer of the divine nature.

They can be compared to a super-intelligence (faith) and a super-will (hope and charity) which permit the soul to enter into contact with God, supreme truth and sovereign good, in a manner and a measure impossible to natural powers. Faith makes us capable of believing firmly the truths revealed by God, having as our motive the authority of God revealing. Hope disposes us to expect with confidence eternal happiness and the means to attain it because of the divine promises, while charity, the most important of the theological virtues, makes us capable of loving God above all things for His own sake and ourselves and our neighbor for love of God.

2. THE RELIGIOUS LIFE AND THE THEOLOGICAL VIRTUES

Let us limit ourselves to the consideration of the religious life in its aspect common to every state of perfection; namely, the evangelical counsels.

Religious poverty is an act of faith in the counsels of the Divine Master which puts the faithful on guard against the grave and humanly fatal dangers of riches and invites them to leave all in order to possess all, that is, to acquire the imperishable goods of the kingdom of God.

It is also an act of hope for the necessities of the body and those of the soul: for the material necessities, insofar as it casts the soul into the paternal arms of divine Providence, which has solemnly promised His assistance through the mouth of Jesus in favor of those who are concerned above all with the glory of God and spiritual goods; for the spiritual needs insofar as, thanks to the spirit of poverty, it has no care or desire except for God and supernatural and eternal goods.

Again poverty is an act of charity for God, Who is preferred to every earthly thing; of charity for one's neighbor for love of God, because the religious, really and spiritually poor, is in the best condition to exercise with disinterestedness, in regard to his neighbor, the two great virtues of justice and charity.

Religious chastity in turn flows out from an act of faith, according to the word of Jesus Himself: "Not all can accept this teaching (that it is better not to marry) but those to whom it has been given (to understand it) ... let him accept it who can." (Mt. 19:12-12)

Charity is related to hope also: to the enlightened hope—which little by little will become intoxicating certitude and concrete authentication—of a soul which, if it renounces all human, though permissible, love, does so because it aspires to the whole-hearted love of God and of its neighbor in God.

Religious chastity, finally, observed in view of its essential end, is identified with charity. The religious gives himself entirely, body and soul, to the Lord to have more facility, surety, and heroism if necessary, to consecrate himself to the glory of God and to the welfare of his neighbor.

Religious obedience is so based on faith that it is no longer itself if this foundation is lacking. Indeed the religious soul obeys because it recognizes and sees God and His will in the legitimate superiors and their commands. It sees God in them as in the consecrated host and in the suffering poor, although for other reasons and in a different way.

It also nourishes hope, sacrificing joyously its personal liberty in view of the great goods assured to him, who, in all humility, always and everywhere, adores and accomplishes the divine will: "He who humbles himself will be exalted." (Lc. 14:11)

Finally, obedience in the concrete is an authentic proof of charity which cannot limit itself to sentiments and projects but manifets itself by its works, as Jesus has proclaimed: "Not he who says 'Lord, Lord' will enter into the kingdom of heaven but he who does the will of my father will enter into the kingdom of heaven." Religious obedience is effective and perfect charity for God and for neighbor out of love for God.

Father Livius Labor writes: "We must insist on the fact that the essence of perfection is in supernatural charity, in its progress, in full dedication of self to God and to the apostolate oriented by obedience. . . . Obedience is not something which hinders or embarasses in the way of the apostolate, but it is the act animated by charity which gives to the whole life the value of a gift. One can never emphasize enough the strict connection between obedience and love." (II, 312s)

3. THE GIFTS OF THE HOLY SPIRIT AND THE INFUSED MORAL VIRTUES

To complete the cortège which accompanies sanctifying grace in the soul the gifts of the Holy Ghost and the supernatural moral virtues are infused at Baptism.

The gifts of the Holy Ghost—which certain theologians, with St. Thomas, say are the permanent effects of the theological virtues—help the soul to live a life of faith, hope, and charity with greater promptitude and generosity. Like the virtues they are a perfecting and an elevation of the natural faculties of the soul: the gifts of wisdom, understanding, of counsel and of knowledge are grafted on to the intellect, being based on the infused virtue of faith, while the gifts of fortitude, piety and fear of God are in the will alongside of the infused virtues of hope and charity.

4. THE RELIGIOUS LIFE; THE GIFTS OF THE HOLY SPIRIT AND
   THE MORAL INFUSED VIRTUES

The infused moral virtues—prudence, justice, fortitude and temperance—render supernatural the acts of all the natural moral virtues, innate or acquired.

The religious life, characterized by the practice of the three evangelical counsels implies necessarily also the greatest use of the gifts of the Holy Ghost and the exercise of the infused moral virtues.

All that we have said above about the religious life in relation to the theological virtues can be repeated here in regard to the gifts of the Holy Spirit, for they are a derivation and a complement of them. If indeed the action of the divine sanctifier of souls unrolls itself in an abundant and irreplaceable way, for which there is no substitute, to maintain the grace of God and to lead to eternal salvation the souls of simple Christians who follow the path of God's commandments, how much more necessary and efficacious will it show itself in those souls which, corresponding to a particular call of God, strive for evangelical perfection in the religious life, and travel by the arduous way of the evangelical counsels!

The virtue of prudence shines forth especially in religious obedience, which gives the certitude that all that is commanded by superiors is in fact better for the soul and that the means offered by its own state of perfection are the most fitting for attaining the general end of the religious life and the specific end of one's own Institute.

The virtue of justice finds its exercise principally in the practice of poverty and obedience. Indeed these virtues look beyond the limits of *duty* to the *rights* of God and of one's neighbor—God Who remains always the absolute master of the person;—the neighbor who should receive in a superabundant fashion from the religious all that is due him for his spiritual and material welfare.

The virtues of fortitude and temperance find an ample field of application in the life of a soul which is vowed to chastity and ruled by the most severe principles of sobriety, interior and exterior mortification and generous and constant sacrifice.

But besides these special considerations which concern each one of the moral virtues in relation to the three evangelical counsels, one can say in a general way that each aspect of the religious life, faithfully lived, contains a continual flowering of these virtues, testifying in the highest degree to a prudent, just, courageous and temperate life.

5. THE RELIGIOUS LIFE AND THE VIRTUE OF RELIGION

The moral virtue of religion has as its object the cult that one must render to God; namely, all the human acts, internal and external, by which a man honors and serves the Lord, practicing the first divine commandment: "You shall have no other God besides Me." It is a virtue which, according to one etymological explanation, binds or rebinds every man—with his interior and exterior acts—to his creator, vowing himself to His cult and service.

Now the religious life is in great harmony with the exigencies of the virtue of religion. Indeed, when it is exercised as it should be it places the whole man in the service of God, of the God-man and of His Mystical Body, for the divine glory and the salvation of souls.

That is why, says St. Thomas, those are called religious by antonomasia who give themselves entirely to the divine service, offering themselves to God as a holocaust.

"They are religious with Christ and in imitation of Christ, the Religious of the Father; with the Church and in imitation of the Church, the mystical spouse of Christ."

In His high-priestly prayer Jesus says: "For them (the apostles) I set apart (that is to say, consecrate) myself (to the service of God) in order that they also be set apart in the truth." Religious are those set apart, consecrated, totally given to the cult of service of God, known and loved in Himself and in one's neighbor.

It is very true that the infidelities of religious, properly so-called, put on a particular malice and the gravity of sacrilege, that is, of profanation of a sacred person.

The world does not understand the religious life and it considers and declares it an unnatural life, unreasonable and absurd.

But in that it shows its false reasoning. Indeed if it is reasonable that man, a creature of God, acknowledge his total dependence on his divine Patron, even by external sentiments and manifestations of adoration, of thanks, of prayer, of devotion, of obedience, etc., it is so much more reasonable and conformable to human nature that the Christian, having become an adopted son of God and brother of Christ, give testimony, as perfectly as possible, of his religion towards the heavenly Father, Who, by means of His only begotten Son, has delivered him from sin, has sanctified him, and can save him and lead him one day into paradise.

And in the upsurge of his religion he can very praiseworthily offer to God not only the obligatory acts but also free acts, flowing out of his love for God, Who is infinitely amiable in Himself and by Himself.

In this way the moral virtue of religion transports us from the natural order to the supernatural order, which perfects nature. And it adds a special value and merit to all the acts of the religious by reason of the religious profession or equivalent act which with the approbation of the Church consecrates to God entirely and permanently the one who makes this profession or accomplishes this act, transferring it to the state of supernatural religion.

Every Christian is consecrated to God by baptism. But the Christian, having become religious, by a kind of second baptism, is doubly and totally a person consecrated to God.

Religious reserve nothing for themselves; they give all and for all time, at least in their personal intention and the disposition of their will. Human life does not exist in one sole moment, and cannot be offered to God in an instant; but by means of profession or an equivalent act the soul accomplishes the prodigy of offering equally all its life to God; by offering the plant it offers also all the fruits, present and future.

"Thanks to this profession or religious oblation," writes Father Llamera, "man frees himself from nature, from the world, from all that is human; frees himself from all, puts himself above all, puts away self, makes himself religious, sacred, divine. Only by a sacrilege of infidelity can he render himself a slave of anyone or of anything, or dispose of himself." (II, 73)

Ancient monastic tradition finds in the religious life a supplement to martyrdom.

CHAPTER VIII

RELIGIOUS MORTIFICATION

1. THE SCIENCE OF LOVE

Appearing to St. Margaret Mary Alacoque, Jesus showed her His open heart and made her read there the science of love. "My heart reigns in immolation, triumphs in humility, and rejoices in unity." (II, 377)

Love of Jesus for the soul and of the soul for Jesus cannot reign unless the soul, cooperating with divine grace, exercises itself constantly in Christian mortification.

Without mortification the evil inclinations of human nature easily pull the soul down. Without being essentially corrupt, as the Protestants erroneously claimed, the soul is forever robbed of its original purity and is inclined towards evil. In order that the new man be born, developed and become perfect, it is necessary that the old man be gotten rid of in the struggle between nature and grace.

"A very ancient monastic tradition," writes Father Olphe Galliard, sees religious profession "as a second baptism, attributing to it a similar purifying power and especially an incorporating value, which makes of the newly professed a soldier of Christ, confirming him anew in the renouncement of the demon by the neophyte and in his attachment to Jesus Christ. . . . The union with the dead and risen Christ is henceforth delineated under the terms of his profession, as an ideal which polarizes his virtuous activities. The symbolism of baptismal water gives place to that of the holy habit which marks the entrance into a new life. The idea of putting on Christ (Gal. 3:27), of the new man (Eph. 4:26) that St. Paul made familiar to the neophytes of his time, takes in the change of habit, the aspect of an evident testimony. The religious affirms it as the one who wishes to be a disciple of Christ, burdened with His cross ready to enter His kingdom with Him. His membership, made visible by the uniform that he wears, urges him to combat without regret, under the banner of the cross." (I, 185s)

2. DIVINE GRACE AND HUMAN NATURE

There is in us the old man, fruit of original sin, tending towards material goods, human honors and the pleasures of the sense. Divine grace wishes to render this tendency helpless, to make it inoffensive, and to eliminate it as much as possible.

Besides the old man there exists in us a soul that is naturally Christian, a good man, endowed more or less with appreciable qualities of body and soul, inborn or acquired. Divine grace wishes to preserve this part of us and put it in its service.

But the divine task is not limited to combatting the evil and preserving and evaluating the good that is in us.

In holy baptism the soul is essentially perfected and elevated by means of the infusion of divine sanctifying grace, the theological virtues, the moral virtues and the gifts of the Holy Spirit. And at every moment of its natural existence, it has at its disposition the special aids of actual grace. Hence a new organism exists in the Christian soul which lives in the friendship with God; the organism of the new man, to which divine grace proposes, as an end to be attained, as far as is humanly possible, the perfection of the heavenly Father.

Hence divine grace does not destroy human nature but perfects it—if the soul collaborates—by a triple action: doing away with obstacles, making use of natural gifts, useful as means to our ultimate end, perfecting the soul by superior gifts. In the case of the religious soul grace tends to form the perfect religious, starting with the good man and the good Christian. And all this grace uses to conduct the soul to the most intimate union with God by means of love.

3. DIVINE LIBERATING GRACE AND COOPERATION OF THE SOUL

Such a cooperation is here considered in relation with the primary office of divine grace in us: to defend us and, within the limits possible, deliver us from the ambushes and attacks of the old man, who, basing himself on the triple concupiscence, seeks to separate us from our last end, God, and to make our ultimate end consist in the very creatures of God, ourselves, others, and created things.

Every Christian soul has the duty of collaborating with

God in the fight against the old man with the goal of avoiding every act which constitutes a sin or an occasion of sin for self or of scandal for one's neighbor. In its mortification it ought to renounce the possession or use of material goods when this possession or use would become even only a danger for self or a scandal for others.

The word and example of Jesus are clear. He has told us that if an eye or a hand is for us an obstacle on the way of perfection, we must cast them far from us, that is to say, make no use of them, mortify them. And He Himself, having the right of exemption from the tribute of the temple, wishes that Peter pay for both of them in order not to scandalize the people who were ignorant of His divine right. (Mt. 5:19; 17:26)

Every Christian soul, moreover, while able to use many pleasant goods (for example, recreation, food) must do so, directing all to the ultimate end, at least implicitly, that is, observing the laws suggested by right reason (for example, to eat and drink in the right measure, time, etc.). The soul will thus confer on its acts at least a very small degree of moral goodness.

Finally a religious soul must not limit itself to avoiding sin or danger for itself and scandal for the neighbor, nor allow licit pleasure to become an end in itself. Vowed to a life of total evangelical perfection and hence of the greatest austerity, it has the obligation of observing also the evangelical counsels and of accomplishing all the acts of mortification that they imply, renouncing effectively, and still more affectively, the possession and use, permitted to other souls, of many material goods.

Mortification finds many occasions for exercise in the religious life; in the obligatory things by reason of the vows, of the common life, of work to be done, etc.; in contingent things, such as infirmities, contrarieties, etc.; in things freely chosen, such as fasts, hair-shirts, watchings, etc., provided one is discreet, avoiding dangerous extravagances, often a source of vain complacency and pride.

If certain bodily mortifications do not seem fitting to many because of the little physical resistance of modern generations who have such great need of nourishment and repose, other forms of obligatory mortification—recommended particularly for our times—are also possible. For example, a more perfect observance of hygiene and of cleanliness; more polish and education in dealing with others; silence and solitude; absence of familiarity with men of the world; flight from effeminate and worldly manners; avoidance of unnecessary journeys. Let us not go on increasing the demands of weak constitutions and give in to the exaggerations of hygiene which under the pretext of health seeks the commodities and pleasures of modern material progress.

"On the question of sleep and nourishment," writes Father Benjamin of the Holy Trinity, "one must trust the judgment of competent Catholic doctors who understand the sense and the exigencies, natural and supernatural, of Christian and religious perfection." (II, 194)

Considering the weakness of physical constitutions, especially of the nervous system, one must avoid excessive tension and agitation. That is why it appeared necessary to assure to all the possibility of a daily rest of eight hours of sleep. . . . "It is necessary to give sufficient rest, especially during the years of study." (Father Idesbald Van Houtryre, O.S.B.) (I, 464)

At the International Congress of Religious, held in Rome in September, 1951, this was said authoritatively: "The hours stolen from sleep sooner or later are paid for. The six or seven hours of sleep which suffice for those in the cloister are insufficient for students or teachers. For these latter groups eight hours of sleep are necessary in order that the nervous system, tired by reason of mental work, can recuperate its energies. Moreover the sleep must be restful; protected from the noise of the street; there should be silence in the corridors and in the cells."

Even the need of sleep, calculated at eight hours, corresponds to a medium, which admits of slight variation in individual cases. Moreover the curve of sleep varies considerably from one subject to another. There are some who sleep soundly very quickly, and whose sleep gradually becomes lighter towards the time of awakening. For these, arising is not difficult, since they cut off only a portion of the lightest sleep. Others, however, sleep soundly only after some hours. They quickly pass over to lighter sleep only to fall into sound sleep again towards the seventh or eighth hours. Rising in the morning takes away from them some of this deep sleep and is therefore very difficult. During the postulancy one must observe the type of sleep of the postulant. Those whose sleep is according to the second type adapt themselves with difficulty to the life of the community without suffering from it; at the least they may be given opportune exceptions.

4. MORTIFICATION AND THE PEOPLE OF THE WORLD

Whoever does not believe in God, or believes only with his mouth, does not accept the Christian doctrine on mortification, for the atheist divinizes man and claims the right to use as he wills all material goods. Such a humanistic-atheistic attitude makes of the natural development and perfection of man the ultimate end of human life.

The radical atheistic humanists say that they do not believe in God and do not wish to believe in Him because to admit the existence of God would mean limiting their own liberty and the possibilities of their own development and perfection.

Theodore Kérier declares: "Even if it could be proved to me mathematically that God exists, I do not wish that He exist, because by limiting me He lessens me." And Nietzche hurls this delirious cry: "God is dead: long live the superman!" (II, 329)

The humanistic practical atheists, even if they say they believe and go so far as to accomplish, by habit or instinct, some external religious practice, do not however accept any moral law and grant to their nature all that it asks for.

There are also humanists, half Christian, who admit the obligation of mortification only insofar as it is necessary to avoid sin, but not to avoid the dangerous or disedifying use of natural goods. For them, having excluded the sinful use of these goods, every other usage is for man a right, or at least a thing absolutely permitted.

Finally there are some who affirm that it is better to use all natural goods in the right way than to renounce them by mortification. And to confirm this statement, they mention certain souls who were sanctified in the world where they lived, for example on a royal throne. Such a statement forgets—as has been said regarding the three evangelical counsels—that ordinarily it is very difficult to keep one's heart detached from natural goods and pleasures when one has the possession and use of them.

The effective renouncement renders the way of evangelical perfection much more expeditious and sure. That is why Jesus proposed to the souls desirous of perfection the evangelical counsels which imply the effective renouncement of certain goods and pleasures to which the human heart is attached with greater facility and tenacity.

5. FROM DEATH COMES LIFE

For a genuine disciple of Christ, and especially for one who has embraced the religious life, the duty and necessity of mortification are beyond discussion. First of all, as we have already said, this is because our nature has been wounded by original sin and inclines towards evil. Left without a bridle it will easily and fatally be entangled in a use of natural goods dangerous for ourselves or scandalous for our neighbor. Likewise we have said that it is necessary to watch over our natural instincts in regard to the use of certain necessary goods—as food, drink, and amusements—in order not to make them an end in themselves but a useful means to our ultimate end.

Thus mortification is a necessary obedience to the commandments and advice of Jesus: "He who does not renounce (at least by affection) all that he has cannot be my disciple. . . . Let him who wishes to follow me deny himself. . . . He who loves his father and mother more than me is not worthy of me. . . . He who does not take up his cross and follow me cannot be my disciple." (Lc. 14:23; Mt. 16:24; 10:37; Lc. 14:27)

There are many other reasons for which we must mortify ourselves. Let us note some of them.

Mortification is a providential purgatory on earth. It is in fact an active purification of the soul which expiates in advance the punishment due to sins pardoned and to attachment to natural goods. In the most generous souls God sometimes accomplishes this purification in a most perfect manner, submitting them to the physical sufferings that the mystics call the night of the senses and of the soul.

On our part mortification is an obligatory contribution to the passion of Christ. For us and for all souls we must do what St. Paul says: "I fill up in my flesh what is lacking to the passion of Christ."

Mortification is an indispensable condition to have a share in the evangelical beatitudes, narrated by St. Luke (ch. 4): "Blessed are the poor. . . . Blessed are those who mourn. . . . Woe to you who are rich. . . . Woe to you who are filled. . . . Woe to you who laugh!"

Mortification is imitation of Jesus. The apostle St. Peter recalls to us in ch. 2 of his first epistle: "Christ has suffered for you, leaving you an example in order that you follow his footsteps."

Our mortification, imitating that of Jesus is a condition for living the life of Jesus. St. Paul has proclaimed it: (II Cor. 4:10) "Always bearing about in our body the dying of Jesus, so that the life also of Jesus may be made manifest in our bodily frame."

To life through death; for us and for our neighbor! From the death of the old man is born life, the true, unique life, the supernatural life of the new man; the life destined to perpetuate itself and to perfect itself in heaven. Thus the integrally Christian humanism, far from destroying man, gives him his full value in time and in eternity better than any other humanism.

CHAPTER IX

RELIGIOUS HUMILITY

1. NOTHING AND LESS THAN NOTHING

Jesus made His privileged saint Margaret Mary read these words in His heart: "My love triumphs in humility." (II, 377) In the humble soul, then, grace triumphs, the love that Christ has for souls triumphs.

Is this so important virtue abused by many and even opposed?

St. Augustine writes that "humility is to be placed on the side of truth, not on that of error." (II, 332)

Humility is truth; it is cult and love of truth: it is truth above all. It is only by the way of truth that the soul and God can meet one another, and that God can work His prodigies of grace in favor of the soul.

The humble soul considers who God is and what it is in relation to God.

What am I by myself in the sight of God? Nothing and less than nothing, for all that there is of good in me—physical and spiritual—is a gift of God, my Creator and my Redeemer; and all that there is of moral evil in me is my work, fruit of my will which has abused its liberty.

I am nothing. And St. Paul says in an address to all: "If anyone thinks himself to be something, whereas he is nothing, he deceives himself." (Gal. 6:3) "What hast thou that thou hast not received? And if thou hast received it why dost thou boast as if thou hadst not received it?" (Cor. 4:7)

I am worse than nothing since I am more or less a sinful soul. St. John affirms this in categorical fashion in his first epistle (I, 8). "If we say that we have no sin, we deceive ourselves."

But if I am nothing, what can I and what ought I to do before God? Kneeling down I can address to Him from the depths of my heart hymns of adoration, of thanks and of praise.

And if I am worse than nothing, what am I and what ought I to do before God? Kneeling down and with my head bowed toward the earth—the word humility comes from *humus*, (earth)— I can and must ask pardon, promise Him sincerely not to sin, protest my firm proposal to make reparation for my sins and to accept in a spirit of expiation all the sufferings and bitterness of life.

I should do all that, and I shall really do it, if I live in truth, profoundly and constantly convinced of being what I am before God: a nothing and worse than nothing.

2. TO JUDGE THE SERVANTS IS A MATTER FOR THE MASTER ONLY

As the meeting of the soul with God should take place in truth in order that it lead to eternal life, to sanctity of the soul and to the glory of God, so the reciprocal relations of the souls must be effected in truth in order that fraternal love be established and reign among them, according to the often repeated desire and will of Christ.

Who am I in the face of my brother? I am not his master, hence I must not judge him. Not being his master nor his judge I must not look upon the doings of my neighbor in order to judge him, for that concerns God.

St. Paul develops these thoughts. (Rom. XIV) "Who art thou to judge another's servant?. . . Why dost thou judge thy brother?. . . we shall all stand at the judgment seat of God . . . every one of us will render an account for himself to God."

But if we must not look at what our neighbor does, what remains for us to see in him? Evidently the other thing which is equally in us, the work of God. Thus seeing in our actions and in those of others the work of God we shall always have more than abundant matter to nourish a sincere spirit of profound humility.

See in this matter the precious teaching of St. Thomas: "Every man, by reason of that which is his own, must consider himself inferior to his every neighbor, by reason of that which is of God in the neighbor. . . . He can believe that there is in his neighbor a good (from God) which he does not have, or that he has in himself an evil that his neighbor does not have. Thus he can place himself below his neighbor by means of humility." (II, 332)

In this way one understands how St. Paul could say to the Christians (Phil. II:2-4) ". . . fill up my joy by thinking alike, having the same charity, with one soul and one mind. Do nothing out of contentiousness or out of vain glory, but in humility let each one look not to his own interests but to those of others."

The virtue of humility does not, of course, prevent the superior from being able and obliged to watch over his subjects, even in that which is their own work, because he does it as one holding the place of God and accomplishing a precise duty.

3. HUMILITY IN THE RELIGIOUS LIFE

To know ourselves; to know the good and the bad that is in us; and to stay in our place before God and neighbor, such is humility.

In the religious life, especially where there is community life, humility finds a thousand occasions each day for exercise and for rooting it in the soul.

Its opposing fault, pride, should not even be mentioned in a truly religious life.

Obedience is, above all, humility, because it is mistrust of self, of one's own point of view, of one's sentiments and desires, and is blind confidence in God through His representatives on earth.

Chastity is humility because, renouncing marriage, it also renounces having a family in which the parents are the rulers, having a right to respect and obedience.

Poverty is humility for it has nothing of its own; in everything it depends on others and has need of permission, even in the use of necessary or useful things.

The common life is humility because it requires the sacrifice of every egoistic instinct, food for pride: pride which would render the common life insupportable if free reign were given to resentments, rancor, antipathies, offensive words, attitudes and gestures of impatience. And all that can be so easily brought about when humility is absent. This virtue alone can awaken, maintain, and increase good understanding and peace among numerous persons differing in character, temperament, education and mentality.

In one word, the religious life places the soul before God and neighbor in the light of humility and truth, which becomes love, service, and devotion, often heroic.

And thus "the fundamental virtue of humility," writes Father Omez, O.P., "is little by little brought back to its true theological conception ... and freed from a certain number of affectations, of meannesses, of caricatures, which render it ridiculous or absurd: as to accuse oneself of faults not committed, or to declare oneself incapable of certain work when one has true ability for it." (II, 182)

4. HE WHO EXALTS HIMSELF IS HUMBLED AND HE WHO HUMBLES HIMSELF IS EXALTED

This is a law proclaimed by the mouth of the prophet Isaias and by Jesus Himself: "I will not give my glory to another." (Is. 42:8) "Whoever exalts himself shall be humbled, and whoever humbles himself shall be exalted." (Mt. 23:12)

The rebel angels, because they were proud, received a severe and irrevocable condemnation.

Our first parents, urged by the demon to revolt, were inexorably chased from their earthly paradise, and it is only by an act of the infinite mercy of God that they did not transmit to their descendants a sentence of definitive condemnation without any possibility of salvation.

Salvation was put at the disposition of souls by the only begotten Son of the Father becoming man and dying on the cross, at the price of an extreme humiliation before God and men. St. Paul says: "Have this mind in you which was also in Christ Jesus, who though he was by nature God, did not consider being equal to God a thing to be clung to, but emptied himself, taking the nature of a slave and being made like unto men. And appearing in the form of man, he humbled himself, becoming obedient to death, even to death on a cross. Therefore God also has exalted him and has bestowed upon him the name that is above every name, so that at the name of Jesus every knee should bend of those in heaven, on earth and under the earth, and every tongue should confess that the Lord Jesus Christ is in the glory of God the Father." (Phil. 2:5-11)

The disciples of Jesus are in the way of salvation and of true glory indicated by his example and by his teaching. "Learn from me, for I am meek and humble of heart." (Mt. 11:29)

At the head of all the humble, after Jesus, stands the humble Mary. To God, Who predestined her to the incomparable dignity of divine mother she answers: "Behold the handmaid of the Lord." Then she chants in her magnificat the glory of the great and all powerful God, of the God Who had regard for her lowliness, of God Who has as a rule the scattering of the proud like feathers to the wind, the putting down from their thrones of the proud, powerful ones and the exalting of the humble.

CHAPTER X

THE COMMON LIFE IN RELIGION

1. ASPECTS OF THE COMMON LIFE

Jesus says to St. Margaret Mary Alacoque: "My love rejoices in unity." (II, 377)

But it is not all the forms of the common life that represent the unity which pleases Jesus.

Likewise not all the aspects of the common life have the same importance and value in the eyes and heart of our Savior.

A primary and non-essential aspect of the common life in religion is living together.

A second aspect, which is essential like the others that will be mentioned, is the possession in common of material goods. The religious earns, no matter under what form, for the community and not for self. All the goods go into the common fund; and the community and no one else provides for the needs of each of the members.

The third aspect of the common life consists in having the same authority and the same laws. All the religious obey the same superior and regulate their lives according to the same disciplinary, spiritual and liturgical rules. The one rule and the constitutions are for all.

A fourth aspect of the common life is the communion of souls, between superior and subjects and between all the members of the religious family, communion of thoughts, sentiments, affections, intentions and works.

This aspect is the most important and also the one which must never be lacking in an authentic common life.

In the history of the states of perfection dwelling together has been the element which we find most varied. Besides strict and perpetual living together, as in the cloistered monasteries, there are also members of secular institutes who do not habitually live together.

Even the common possession of material goods takes on a less severe character in many communities, with the concession of the right of property called radical, and sometimes with a certain liberty of disposing of some possessions.

Even the community of authority and of law can admit of exceptions. For example, a religious who is a bishop no longer lives, like his confreres, the common life under its first three aspects. However, he remains a member of his religious family to which its most important aspect binds him.

Father Labor writes of this: The common life "consists not so much in always doing all things collectively, as in having a mutual, true, deep and supernatural love, and a profound and sincere attachment to the spiritual and apostolic family of which one is a part. One must not stop with a materialistic concept of the common life, but strive to establish as perfectly as possible the communion of souls who live the same ideal, who put together their experiences, who pray, work, study, suffer and rejoice together and discuss together the best means to gain the victory over their souls. . . . It is important to have a right idea and a reasonable realization of the common life, in the sense of a really family-like atmosphere, style and tone, elevated not by the petty sentiments characteristic of the bourgeoisie, but by sentiments of friendship, open to a generous spirit of service which will be realized in an accumulation of indispensable aids of a spiritual, psychological, cultural, physical, economical, and social nature." (II, 311s, 314)

2. LIVING TOGETHER IN THE NAME OF JESUS

Hence the most important and irreplaceable element of the common life of religious is constituted by its last aspect: the communion of thoughts, affections, sentiments, plans of action and works.

Indeed, this may seem impossible and improbable, but it is the element that is most neglected in theory and in practice.

Dwelling together is wisely desired by the Church for the majority of communities.

The three other elements, on the contrary, are derived from the three evangelical counsels. The common possession of goods is an exigency of the practice of evangelical poverty. The common seat of authority and of laws flows from the practice of obedience. The last element has its principal source in the practice of evangelical chastity, which, as was said when treating of this virtue, should diffuse itself in a constant, generous and sincere fraternal love, which transforms the religious family into a true family in name and in fact and thus realizes the promise of Jesus: .... "There is no one who has left house, or brothers, or sisters, or mother, or father, ... for my sake and for the gospel's sake, who shall not receive now in the present time a hundredfold as much." (Mk. 10:29-30)

St. Basil the Great and other holy fathers have emphasized the greater advantages of the common life in religion.

Such a life in common is less exposed to the dangers of the moral order and less subject to the possible illusions and to the wants of the solitary life, for it offers to all religious the material, cultural, moral and spiritual assistance of all other members of the community, consecrated to the same ideal of Christian perfection.

Moreover the common life offers hundreds of occasions in which one can practice patience, humility, etc., which are eminently social virtues and in the eremitical life remain in the state of good intentions.

"Men," writes Father Carpentier, S. J., "have been created and especially recreated (redeemed) to form a family, which reproduces the image and gives participation in the felicity of Trinitarian love."

It realizes the desires of the heart of Jesus: "Yet not for these (the apostles) only do I pray, but for those also who through their word are to believe in me, that all may be one, even as thou, Father, in me and I in thee; that they also may be one in us, ... I in them and thou in me; that they may be perfected in unity." (Jn. 17:20-23)

Then the Church can chant the hymn of fraternal love which unites all in Christ and in God. "Where there is charity there is love, there is God. . . . It is the love of Christ which has united us."

This hymn recalls to us the promise of Jesus: "Where there are two or three united in my name, I am in the midst of them." (Mt. 18:20)

The first Christian community lived in such a union: "They were one heart and one soul," the Acts of the Apostles tells us (ch. 4). And regarding true religious families St. Augustine says: "Many bodies, but not many souls."

3. THE RIGHT MEDIUM BETWEEN TWO NON-CHRISTIAN SYSTEMS OF THE SOCIAL LIFE

Two cities, writes St. Augustine, dispute for the empire of the world, the city of God, of the good, and the city of the demon, of the wicked. The first is founded on social love, that is, on charity, the second is based on private love, that is egoism. If the Good which is loved (God) is common to all, unity is assured; if it is particular (earthly goods), dissension is inevitable. (I, 244s)

The celebrated interpretation given by the holy doctor to the history of humanity is always valid.

Two non-Christian systems of social life dispute today for the empire of the world, the liberal and the communistic, while outside of Christianity one calls in vain for a just regime of the democratic community which assures the duties and rights of all with an equal distribution of earthly and human goods.

The liberal system claims for all individuals the greatest possible liberty; thus it favors egoistic individualism, it diminishes and almost annuls the function of authority which ought to safeguard the welfare of all against the cupidity of some.

The communistic system goes to the other extreme; it gives all rights to the community and reduces the individuals to a mass of numbers, leveled and irresponsible, thus divinizing, in practice, the authority which remains in the hands and at the service of certain ones.

These two systems, for different reasons, are not in harmony with the Christian system, which, presupposing faith in God, and justice and charity towards all men, safeguards on the one hand the rights of individuals and on the other hand protects the exigencies of the common good in relation to particular goods. Thus the Christian system gives their due to the authority and to the subjects, by means of a common regime, truly democratic.

In the Christian regime of social life there is harmony, concord and collaboration because, the material goods being distributed among individuals according to equity and charity, the souls find themselves united in the search for a possession of the infinite and eternal God, the common good.

In the non-Christian regions, on the contrary, there can be no harmony, concord and collaboration because egoism, on the one hand, hinders the exercise of charity and of social justice, for each one barricades himself in his own goods and seeks to appropriate those of others; and, on the other hand, the materialistic conception of life does not permit souls to find themselves united in God, the inexhaustible good, but embitters more and more the hate and struggle between the rich and the poor.

The form of social life in force in the religious state is the best application of the Christian system. It is in fact the fusion of the individuals in the same fraternal spirit and in the same apostolic action to attain a common ideal. It is the respect accorded to particulars, in harmony with the good of the community. It is the concrete recognition —in God, Lord and Father of all—of mutual rights and duties. It is the assigning of his post to each one; the collaboration of all for each and of each for all.

Naturally, a system of Christian social life—and *a fortiori* a religious system—cannot please a non-Christian world, which considers it, wrongly, as contrary to the rights of the individual or to the legitimate exigencies of the collectivity.

4. DIFFICULTY OF THE COMMON LIFE

It is not easy to live perfectly the common life which we have just described. It was not without reason that St. John Berchmans said: "My greatest penance is the common life." (I, 227)

The most frequent sore spot of this life—not to speak of the faults against fraternal charity—are the excessive dispensations of superiors who are too condescending, the exceptions that the subjects, impatient towards all discipline, claim, and the too easily granted indults of exclaustration and secularization.

There are superiors too indulgent toward human weakness, and perhaps also desirous for themselves of greater liberty, who give dispensations with extreme facility, without sufficiently taking account of the consequences of their acts on the life of the community.

It happens that those who are too easily dispensed urge those who are not dispensed to seek, without sufficient motive, the same favors as well as others. Thus the general level of observance is lowered and laxity is favored among all.

If things do not go that far, there is a sort of psychological scandal among those who do not make use of dispensations; a sort of inevitable moral discomfort which certainly does not favor the increase of fervor in the community.

That is so true that many propose the isolation of those who are habitually dispensed, in houses reserved for them, or at least in a section of the same building.

But a still greater sore of the common life consists in dispensations which are granted in an arbitrary way to lax or even strayed members, who are not punished as they should be by superiors who are too weak.

For example: one is absent from the common exercises; another has spending money at his free disposal; a third receives presents and in turn gives presents to others, and so on.

It is clear that such examples finally become contagious because evil is more easily imitated than good. Then one will have a common life which has gone astray.

Moreover, a great danger to the common life—among so many others—is furnished by indults of exclaustration and secularization because of re-entry into the community, abandoned temporarily, of exclaustrated religious, or again —by a special new indult—of religious secularization.

It is not difficult to imagine that those who have come back find it hard to take up again the rhythm of a truly regular life. They will be like a dead weight in the bosom of the community, drawing the others down rather than raising them up.

For this reason greater strictness from competent authority is asked by many in this matter.

We must again recall a final negative element of regular observance: the practical difficulty of eliminating quickly from community life those who unfortunately must be sent away because they are the bad sheep capable of contaminating the whole flock.

Regarding these last three causes of laxity in the common life, Father Quatember, S.O.C., writes: "Dispensations and exemptions are given with too much indulgence or complicity, plagues of the common life, which take away its vigor and splendor. There are religious who seek to obtain these exemptions by means of indults from the Holy See: absences from the religious house, temporary exclaustration or secularization. The Holy See, when the conditions are observed and the opinion of competent authority obtained, concedes the indults under the form of commission so that superiors, according to their good pleasure and their conscience, may grant or refuse the favor. But it is extremely regrettable that superiors do not inform the Holy See exactly. It happens that a favor is granted when, in conscience, it should not be and when the Holy See, if better informed, would certainly not have granted it.

There are, however, cases where it is really necessary for the common good to send away a religious who imperils the common observance through weakness... or moral or physical incapacity. It is only as a last resort that one should be sent away." The author then enumerates various cases of physical or psychical sicknesses, of malice or lack of good will—cancer of the common life—and concludes: "It seems to us very desirable and opportune that the Holy See open, for this purpose, another issue... distinct from the method of judiciary process, in order that religious who habitually fail in regard to the common life, may be dismissed by administrative way, observing all conditions ... to avoid abuses on both sides."

He concludes, designating the chapter of faults—clinic and sanitorium of the common life—as a very efficacious remedy for the restoration and conservation of regular observance, provided that such a practice be not reduced "to a ceremony without soul and without effect," but that it be truly "a preventive remedy against the negligence of the common life, a reparation and expiation of infractions which are committed against it." (II, 241-244)

CHAPTER XI

MEANS OF RELIGIOUS PERFECTION

1. HE WHO WILLS THE END WILLS THE MEANS

It is obligatory to have serious and efficacious recourse to the means of perfection because it is ordained or counseled by the particular laws of each congregation or by the general laws of the Church.

On the one hand, the difficulty that one meets on the way of his own sanctification demands this use of means which obtains for the soul light and strength necessary to know and realize the good.

The apostolate, finally, is not possible without an intense interior life, which finds its nourishment in these means.

Without them the apostolate will be superficial, based on mere natural means instead of being based, above all, on prayer—the apostolate of the knees, so to say—and on sacrifice.

A soldier who does not know how to use his weapons is of no value, neither to himself nor to others. One can say as much of one who wishes to attain intimate union with God by means of charity and who, through love of

God, wishes to give himself to the service of his neighbor, victoriously overcoming the rude combats of the spirit.

2. IN ANY STATE OF PERFECTION LIFE CAN ONLY BE ACTIVE

In regard to the religious life much is said and spoken of the contemplative, the active, and the mixed life. Let us speak of these also, and let us explain the ideas and principles exactly.

The contemplative life, entirely interior, seeks for union of the soul with God, in detachment from the world, in silence and interior recollection.

To live as one ought it is necessary to avoid the possible perils which flourish on the surface, such as monotony, which can put the soul to sleep; too much work, physical and intellectual, which can distract it from heavenly things; spiritual laziness, which leads the spirit to a fatal quietism or to a mechanical pharisaism consisting of external observances.

The life of contemplation, lived in an authentic way, is very precious in the sight of God and for the good of souls, God manifests Himself lovingly to the soul, He draws it to Himself by a reciprocal gift, entire and lasting. The soul, filled with God, gives itself then to other souls especially by prayer, sacrifice, and example. Thus it transforms itself into a sort of resonance box where all human miseries, physical and intellectual, find a sympathetic echo.

The Carmelite Father, Gabriel of St. Mary Magdalene, asks: "Is not the evident advantage of the contemplative life from a personal point of view offset by inconvenience from the social and apostolic point of view?" He answers with the words of the saints and of Pope Pius XI: "St. Therese of the Child Jesus, proclaimed by Pope Pius XI as the patroness of all the missions, in her interior life of the apostolate was inspired directly, and explicitly by this doctrine of the mystical doctor (St. John of the Cross). 'A little pure love, that is, of a soul which has attained union with God, is more useful to the church than all other works put together . . .' Pius XI, the great pope of the exterior apostolate, of the missions and of Catholic action, in his encyclical letter on the missions, rightly recalls his special esteem for the purely contemplative life. "Those who undertake the office of prayer and of continual mortification contribute more to the increase of the Church and to the salvation of souls than those who cultivate the field of the Lord by their activity." (III, 100s)

The contemplative life is not understood and esteemed in the world which understands and appreciates a dynamic life, full of external activity, a life that is materially productive. It is a question of point of view. That of God is not that of men who are deprived of the Christian view of human life.

But God, as though He wished to take a manifest revenge on the materialistic world, still today continues to call souls of the elite to the contemplative life. In France, for example, it has been noticed that these vocations have made noticeable increase.

The active religious life applies itself to the good of one's neighbor in the multiple and ever more numerous works of the apostolate.

But the active life, to be religious—here is an important point which ought to be well formulated in order to avoid pernicious equivocations—can be neither exclusively nor in a predominant way active in the sense that we have indicated above.

One could call it the active life insofar as its exterior organization has been willed, conceived and realized in view of works of the exterior apostolate.

But one cannot call it such in this sense that it could do without, or almost do without, the interior life, which is the soul of every true and fertile apostolate. Love of neighbor must flow from love of God, it must conform and unite itself to charity. Jesus has saved the world especially by His passion and death.

Therefore in the intimate exigencies of the active religious life there enters a minimum of contemplative life, which makes sanctification possible for the soul and renders it apt for the exterior apostolate.

Whence the practical consequence of extreme importance: even and especially in the active religious life, because of the particular dangers and difficulties that it entails, it is necessary and obligatory to recur in a diligent and attentive way to the well-known and worthily appreciated means of religious perfection.

Whence the other consequence already announced: in any state of religious perfection life cannot be merely active. It will necessarily be purely contemplative or mixed, that is, contemplative and active.

This mixed life is nothing else than an integral Christian and religious life.

It is not easy to maintain the equilibrium between the active and contemplative life as the saints knew how to do: but it is indispensable that it be maintained by giving the primacy to the contemplative life, if one wishes to avoid the dangers for the soul and its apostolate.

A page merits to be transcribed here. It is a testimony of unrest and almost of regret from Father Gabriel of St. Mary Magdalen: "If we have need of more active forces, let us render more efficacious those which already exist, especially by aiding the poor Sisters to live a life of greater union with God. I can give testimony of this: Sisters who lead an active life are often deprived of sufficient exercises of piety; they are frequently plunged into material work and are insufficiently prepared for their apostolic work. . . .

They all embrace the religious life with a sincere desire for self-sanctification, but often, after some years, they convince themselves that sanctity is not for them, precisely because they feel they are helped so little. I am firmly convinced that we have in the Sisters great powers for the apostolate which are lost because they are not nourished by the interior life. And if we wish our secular institutes to flourish, in which . . . the specific purpose of the apostolate has awakened the other general good of perfection and of sanctity, we must seek to organize them so that there also the interior life be nourished abundantly. And I would say, not in any way whatsoever: if we wish that the apostolic harvest be full—it should be so in the Institutes created precisely for the apostolate—it is necessary that among them the apostolate be carried out in all its plenitude, not only under the form of external activity, but also of interior prayer and immolation. Thus I believe that the life which should inspire the secular institutes is the mixed rather than the active. And remember this:

to transform the active life into the mixed it is not sufficient that any kind of union of the interior and of the
active life be effected, but it is necessary that the interior
life be so intense that it concentrate the soul in the search
for God and maintain all external activity under the influence of the internal life of prayer and union with God."
(II, 103)

Father Jambart, S.J. emphasizes this last thought. He
writes: "The doctrine of St. Thomas on the superiority of
the mixed life is sometimes badly understood. For the holy
Doctor it is a question of a life above all contemplative,
which, without diminishing, communicates spiritual riches
to others. . . . In our days certain small congregations claim
ingenuously to have the mixed life, and find themselves
consequently in the most perfect category of religious
institutes.

In reality it is a question of congregations which had
to introduce certain exercises of piety, rigorously required
by canon law (can. 595), but who pass nearly the whole
day in occupations which by their nature are worldly:
teaching children the alphabet, writing and arithmetic. . .
overseeing pupils, sewing, ironing, mending . . . taking care
of the aged or of the sick, cooking, etc. It would be very
wrong to despise these things; but they are far from the
contemplative life and even from the true mixed life, in
spite of many prayers fitted into the day (supposing that
one is always faithful). . . . Many congregations lead an
active life, a very active life today, too active. They are
in danger of not safeguarding even the minimum, required
by the church, of the contemplative life. . . . I am told that
one superior openly suppressed, for some months, nearly

all the exercises of piety of his subjects (leaving them only the Mass) to facilitate for them the preparation of certain examinations!" (II, 116)

The following is from Father Henry of St. Therese: "As to the institutes of the active life I have strong doubts in the theoretic exactitude and the practical opportunity of this name. In theory no religious institute is exclusively or even predominantly, active. Every apostolic activity must overflow from the superabundance of the interior life. . . . And then how can we distinguish between an institute of the active life and another of the mixed life? In practice, by dint of repeating that certain institutes are not of the mixed but of the active life . . . one has often had the result that these institutes in their entirety or in many of their members have neglected the interior life seriously to give themselves to an activism not very supernatural. . . . We must recall and vigorously affirm that these institutes, said to be of the active life, are in reality of the mixed life; and that for them also, that holds which is true of every Christian apostolate in general, that is to say, that the principal part is union with God, sought in the life of prayer and recollection." (II, 169s)

3. PRINCIPAL MEANS OF NOURISHING THE INTERIOR OR CONTEMPLATIVE LIFE

a) Meditation

In order to explain the concept of meditation, it will be useful to see what natural meditation or contemplation is.

I view leisurely a panorama, a work of art, thus I contemplate and meditate; I experience an intimate satisfaction and raise myself to noble and high thoughts.

If I view a person who attracts me by his beautiful qualities, I contemplate him. In contemplating him I love him, and in loving him I wish to contemplate him. If this person is far from me I continue to contemplate and to love him, I recall him to my mind, I contemplate and meditate on him making use of my memory and imagination.

Religious meditation or contemplation has as its object God, the God-man, the Blessed Virgin, heaven, all that can and ought to interest the soul, made for God, supreme truth and sovereign good.

Hence we can define contemplation as a personal and spiritual contact with God, a union of our soul with the infinite being, worthy of being known and loved above all things.

But since God is not present to us in a sensible way, the soul contemplates Him by making use of the imagination. By contemplating and meditating by the light of reason and faith, it feels itself sweetly inflamed with love.

The importance of meditation is thus defined by Father Benjamin of the Holy Trinity: "Mental prayer, or better, union with God which is its center, is an end in itself and is not ordained to any other thing." (II, 190)

A vast and solid field of meditation is offered us by Holy Scripture, where God Himself reveals Himself to man, by the holy liturgy of the Church, the mystical spouse of Christ and our mother, an imposing and ever recurring summary of the principal truths of our religion, efficacious representation of the mysteries of God, of Christ, of the

Virgin, of the angels and saints; the mystical body of Christ and the communion of saints, the kingdom of God in the triple society of the children of God: the church militant, suffering and triumphant; the last things: death, judgment, heaven and hell; and every reality or truth which can nourish the heart and the spirit in view of our apostolate and of our own perfection.

In order to meditate fruitfully one must have a method. Spiritual authors give abundant counsels on this matter. But every soul, having its own characteristics, its personal divine vocation, must strive to find, with the advice of a director, a method adapted to its character, to the various states and moments of its spiritual life. It must not, however, make itself a slave of the method.

The choice of a meditation book has its importance; many are superficial, lacking a solid dogmatic basis; too many are entangled in a wrongly understood piety, consisting of empty sentimentalism, of images and sentiments more or less sweetened.

Regarding this matter Father Henry of St. Therese writes: "Many books of meditation which are in the hands of religious have ... an activist orientation. Instead of insisting on the loving contemplation of God in the mysteries of faith, whence the flood of love gushes forth spontaneously over the moral life of the religious and on his apostolate, more often the mystery serves them as a pretext for launching forth immediately into moral applications. By nourishing oneself with such meditations one will know well what he has to do, but one will not have stored away love to accomplish the apostolate supernaturally." (II, 172)

The Carmelite Father, Benjamin of the Holy Trinity, gives us this idea: "In practice meditation has too often been made an exercise of moral reform for the religious. Evidently this reform must not be excluded from prayer, but is merely a consequence of it. It is in the personal contact with God that the soul best discovers its faults as well as the demands of the divine liberality." (II, 190)

For the same reasons it is also important to adopt for meditation in common the reading of one or several points taken from a common book and to dim the light a little. Today the opposite idea seems to prevail; one tends to safeguard the free and spontaneous initiative of the soul, which at certain times might prefer—in place of the common book or of the one that a person habitually uses— a different reading or a prayer savored for a long time, or the simple state of the presence of God, in a humble and childlike abandon.

b) Spiritual Reading

We must only repeat here what was said of meditation: that the books be well chosen, that preference be given to Holy Scripture, to the lives of the saints, to classical treatises on the spiritual life and religious perfection, to catechism and to the rules and constitutions.

Thus the soul can acquire a good general theological and ascetic culture, which can be of much aid in the ways of the spiritual life. Of course God can supply—He has done so many times—for the incapacity and involuntary ignorance of simple souls with a good will.

Then one will see less often the sad picture of the religious soul showing forth a mediocre anemic life, because its ideas on the spiritual life are incomplete, vague and confused.

Thus one can be better prepared, in contacts with other people, to refute errors, to clarify doubts, to destroy prejudices and superstitions.

Concerning Holy Scripture as a subject of daily reading, privately or publicly, it is useful to recall what Pope Pius XII, in his encyclical letter "Divino Afflante Spiritu", recommended to all Christians and their families. How communities and religious souls should feel a great need of it! But in an inquiry recently made in a considerable number of religious houses it was shown that even the Pope is little heard in these quarters. More than one author —for example, Father Middendorf, S.C.I. (II, 226)—proposes that the Church intervene and make this reading obligatory, which has always been held in great honor and esteem in monastic tradition, and which, thanks to God, even among the laity, finds today an extraordinary ardor of spirit and of heart, in the desire to draw living waters from the sources themselves of divine revelation. Of course this reading is regulated by someone who can give opportune directives, in harmony with the specific spirit and purpose of each congregation.

Only familiarity with the Bible, especially with the Gospel, will revive in religious the authentic evangelical and divine spirit. It would not be easy, for example, to fail so frequently in the Gospel method of fraternal correction, so clearly indicated by Jesus.

A copy of the Bible, sufficiently annotated, should always be found at the disposition of every religious, just as a daily missal or other suitable book which makes the holy liturgy intelligible and lovable. Even here the example of the laity is instructive.

St. Therese of the Child Jesus, enraptured at first by the "Imitation of Jesus Christ," was afterwards exalted by the wonderful discoveries that she made in the Gospel, in the Epistles of St. Paul. From one sentence of Jesus she drew her whole spirituality: her "Little Way of Spiritual Infancy."

c) General and particular examination of conscience

Certain ones consider the examination of conscience as an act of accusation, as though it were deplorable ego-centrism of those spiritually ill. They say that God is not a calculator and does not wish us to lose precious time counting sins and imperfections but that He wishes us to be spontaneous and simple in our spiritual life.

Such an accusation marks a subtle and insidious form of self-love which refuses to recognize personal faults and failings, or does not feel disposed to become seriously oc-cupied with the purification of the soul and growth in virtue.

Examination of conscience is very useful. But it must not be reduced to a stereotyped and material statistic, mechanically made, nor to an excessive self-consideration. On the contrary it should be a diligent search of the in-tentions which underlie our actions and which give the principal value to our acts. It ought to be a confident opening of the soul to the action of divine grace.

To this end certain formularies of examination of conscience are reviewed, exposed and adapted to various classes of persons. It is only in this way that the examination of conscience will attain its end—to know oneself in order to correct oneself.

d) Manifestation of conscience and spiritual direction

In ancient times, the Abbot was, as the word implies, the spiritual father of the other monks, to whom they addressed themselves spontaneously and with unlimited confidence, and opened their souls to receive counsel, comfort, and peace. And the Abbess was truly the spiritual mother of the nuns.

Thus things went on more or less until about the 16th century when manifestation of conscience to the superior was made obligatory. But it soon became the occasion of abuses and spiritual damage, especially in the religious institutes of women.

Hence in 1890 the Church abolished the obligation.

Today canon 530 prescribes what is to be done in this matter. The subjects may freely and spontaneously open their heart to the superior; it is fitting that they go to him with filial confidence.

It is to be desired that, in the relations of subjects to superiors, the supernatural dispositions of soul, impregnated with the spirit of faith and obedience, should be reborn. Then, if the superiors know how to gain the confidence of their subjects with a paternal or maternal kindness, the exhortation of the church can be more easily realized, tending to save and evaluate for the good of the subjects the spiritual functions of the superior in the religious family.

It is useful to recall that the manifestation of conscience, when it concerns sins, doubts, anxieties of spirit, and so many other intimate questions, though always licit on the part of the subject (even if made to a non-ecclesiastic superior) is not always advisable. It will be the role of a prudent superior to permit, prevent, or limit it.

In any case the soul will not walk with surety and facility in the way of religious perfection if it does not entrust itself to a wise and experienced guide for counsel. This guide may be—and usually is—the ordinary confessor and the spiritual father, but, as has been said, he may also be the one who holds the place of the heavenly Father in the religious family.

Father Benjamin of the Holy Trinity writes: "Without an enlightened and constant spiritual direction it is ordinarily very difficult for religious souls to apply their convictions in practice and to use profitably the means of the spiritual life. It is to be deplored that many religious do not have a spiritual director. The result is that, traveling alone on the way of perfection, they make little progress, and if they are young, they form themselves without knowing themselves and with the pitiful result of not acquiring the characteristics which are the mark of their institute." (II, 189)

Father Ghezzi of St. Francis Xavier asks: "What is the purpose of the manifestation of conscience? It is first of all for the spiritual advantage of the religious. One of the most fatal illusions in this world is to think that one is sufficient for himself. To seek to direct oneself alone, without taking counsel from prudent persons—no matter what may be the field of activity—is the cause of many mistakes and the occasion of going astray. In the spiritual order the danger is greater because the work of one's own sanctification is the most arduous of all, because the passions, especially self-love, can lead one into error and because the devil is very eager that it be so, whether for hindering the profit of the religious himself or for impeding the good of so many souls. The second purpose of manifesting one's conscience is to obtain for the religious tranquility of soul. The idea that the spiritual father, knowing the religious well, can give advice appropriate for his progress is a source of great peace and of true happiness for the good religious."

The same author explains the disposition with which the manifestation of conscience should be made, namely, with a right intention, humility and sincerity. The material of such a manifestation includes vocation, temptations, character, fraternal charity, rules, and practices of piety. Afterwards he distinguishes from manifestation of conscience the disciplinary account of one's actions, that is, "the manifestation of his conduct to his superior concerning his external and disciplinary life, the faults being excluded." The purpose of this he expresses as follows: "To give to the superior the possibility of knowing each one in order that he can guide himself in the conferring of appointments." He explains the matter of this manifestation as the vows, the common life, charity, inclinations. According to his advice one is to be advised to make a manifestation of conscience only to the spiritual father, even if the subject may make it to the superior, when this latter is a priest. (II, 697-701)

The necessity of spiritual direction is inculcated efficaciously by Father Marchetti, S.J., who shows in the natural order the need of parents for a child, of teachers for a student, of a guide for mountain climbers, of a doctor for the sick, of a lawyer and a judge for the accused or the offended. He affirms that it is not to be advised that spiritual direction be carried on ordinarily by correspondence. (II, 702s)

Finally the Capuchin Father, Virgil of St. Vitus, treating of the manifestation of conscience, refers among other things to the causes that can hinder it, and enumerates the following: ignorance of what it really is; an aversion (not always explicable) towards the spiritual father; fear of being scolded and corrected (which can cause one to be silent and even to lie); shame, fed by the fear of being badly judged by the spiritual director; the conviction that to relate to others one's good or bad affairs is something almost ridiculous. He then describes different types of souls, concerning the manifestation of conscience: some make a manifestation only rarely or only in part; some wish to have explanations and counsel; some wish to take revenge on the devil, who turns them away from it; some see Christ in the spiritual director; some do it through a spirit of mortification; some wish to increase in themselves grace and merits; sometimes there is no clear reason; some are convinced by themselves or by others; some are pushed by an irresistible internal movement; finally, but rarely, some find a certain taste (good or bad) for it. (II, 717s)

e) Recollection and spiritual exercises

Today especially these two means, if they are used with fervor and method, are among the most efficacious for the progress of the soul and the higher spiritual level of the communities.

Regarding spiritual exercises—and proportionately this holds for recollection—the Carmelite Father Benjamin of the Holy Trinity writes: "The course of spiritual exercises must be a time of greater recollection during which, under the eye of God, religious souls are intimately conscious of the demands of their vocation and of divine grace in their regard. They are a stopping place on the way of life where the soul may acquire renewed strength in intimate contact with God." Few sermons, and few pious practices in common, Father Benjamin advises, but much recollection and silence and a great personal fervor to find oneself again before the Lord, to examine oneself and to pray. (II, 193)

Father Veuthey is of the same mind. "Let the time of silence, of personal reflection, of reading and private prayer be increased, and let the sermons and external distractions be diminished; the salutary fruits of spiritual exercises will gain thereby." (II, 233)

f) The sacraments

The sacraments are channels of grace. Confession and communion ought to be, especially for the religious soul, irreplaceable instruments of purification, of strength, of illumination and of union with God.

g) *Prayer*

Prayer is the means willed by Jesus for obtaining from Him the actual graces we need. Prayer is the admission of our poverty and the act of confidence and abandon to God.

Preferred above private prayer is that which is public, especially the liturgy, which is the prayer of the Church, that is, of the mystical Christ. Through this prayer we unite ourselves to Him and to His spouse, asking for ourselves grace and salvation from the Father.

Many wishes have been expressed concerning the Divine Office. In the congregations which prescribe its recitation one should strive for a good understanding and devout recitation of it. If it is recited in Latin all should be able to understand this language or an authentic translation should be made into the vernacular to facilitate its understanding.

Where the Divine Office is not prescribed one might ask whether it would be profitable to introduce the recitation of the little hours of the breviary or a shorter office. The suggestion has also been made for many religious houses that Prime be recited in the morning and Compline in the evening.

As to private prayer, personal or in common, today it is insisted that we avoid those that are too long, or accumulations of prayers without any order, which give signs of indiscretion and sometimes superstition. One should eliminate all texts that are sentimental, superficial, or of a romantic character.

The great Origen says that prayer is the "respiration of the soul in God." (II, 208) Hence let us make the soul breathe pure air containing plenty of oxygen.

h) Work

Even work, no matter what kind it may be, becomes a means of personal sanctification if it is spiritualized by the right intention and by the spirit of penance and of charity towards one's neighbor.

It constitutes the primary means of subsistence for religious—as for all men— excepting the particular laws of some communities.

On this point Father Gallen, I.M.C., writes: "The activity which in our times seems to be the best adapted to assure the principal reverence of religious institutions appears to be the personal work of its members. Communism, whether one likes it or not, has infiltrated at least some of its tenets into the masses, and these latter no longer appreciate a state of life where productive work is not the basis of the life of each one. We understand here any kind of work: intellectual, teaching, or manual work for those who cannot leave the cloister." (I, 655)

Father Maurus de Grizzana expresses his thought in this pithy sentence: "The purest form of poverty in the religious life is to live from one's own work." (II, 176)

It is urgently demanded by the material and spiritual necessities of the society so violently attacked by the enemies of God. It then becomes our apostolate, that is, love of God in one's neighbor and of one's neighbor in God.

i) *Recreation*

Let no one be astonished to see recreation placed here among the means of religious perfection. The soul and body form an inseparable and interdependent whole. And the soul must grant to the body the necessary rest if it wishes faithful and diligent service from it.

Recreation should truly attain its end, which is the real restoration of soul and body. Certain types of recreation, as for example, sitting around the superior in conversation, are ordinarily not recommended. In certain cases it could be useful and agreeable to do some light manual labor, to take a walk, or to play some game.

One should beware of vacations and furloughs lest in giving recreation to the body harm be done to the soul. Vacations should not be spent with the family or in houses of the laity because the constant and prolonged contact with worldly persons—it makes little difference that they are relatives, friends or acquaintances—puts the soul in the frequent occasion of failing in its duties and of assimilating little by little the spirit of the world.

4. WORDS OF THE POPE

These words were spoken on July 7, 1947, the occasion being the canonization of Blessed Garicoits and Bichier des Ages: "Superficial persons will ask by what miracle could the immense extent and the fathomless depth of their external activity be reconciled with the interior recollection of their eminently spiritual and contemplative life. But why speak of reconciliation? Reconciliation of the flame of their zeal, which propagates the fire outside, and the furnace of charity whence it is ignited? Between the splendor that they shed around them and the infinite light of which they bore the reflections? . . . Be deaf to the temptation to sacrifice your religious life and your personal sanctification to the apostolate. This would be like taking from the tree the blossoms scarcely open in order to make a bouquet, and afterwards to look for fruit on the branches that had been robbed." (I, 25s)

In his exhortation to the Catholic clergy of the world on September 23, 1950, Pope Pius XII, said: "Everyone knows, dear sons, that it is not possible. . .to imitate the admirable examples of our Divine Master without the aid of grace and recourse to the instruments of grace which He Himself has put at our disposition; recourse which is all the more necessary, since the degree of perfection which we must attain is higher and since the difficulties flowing from our nature inclining us to evil, are more serious. . . . As a fundamental principle of Christian perfection St. Paul gives us the precept: 'Put on the Lord Jesus Christ'. . . . But to put on Christ implies a long and arduous work which places the soul in a state of victim so that it can intimately share in the sacrifice of Jesus. This arduous and assiduous work is not accomplished by empty wishes and is not fulfilled by desires and promises, but it must be an indefatigable and persevering exercise . . . ; exercise of piety, exercise of penance; act of charity . . . a will active for the struggle and fatigue.

The Church exhorts us above all to meditation. From negligence of this practice there is born tepidity of spirit, from which follows lessening and languor of piety. . . . That is why it must be affirmed that no other means has the particular efficacy of meditation and its daily practice cannot be replaced.

One must not separate mental prayer from vocal prayer. . . . One must, however, remember that piety and the fervent spirit of prayer is of greater value than multiplied prayers. This ardent spirit of prayer is more than ever necessary today since materialism has invaded souls and virtue is exposed to dangers of every kind. . . .

Moreover, it is opportune to make another recommendation; in the beginning and while making progress in the spiritual life do not trust yourself, but with simplicity and docility ask the aid of Him, who, with a wise moderation, can guide your soul. . . . Without this prudent guide of conscience it is very difficult ordinarily to follow worthily the movements of the Holy Spirit and of divine graces."

In the Apostolic Constitution, "Sponsa Christi," November 21, 1950, Pope Pius XII writes: "All, not excluding the contemplative religious, are obliged to do work— manual or intellectual—not only by the natural law, but also by the obligation of penance and satisfaction." Moreover work is the ordinary means which keeps the soul from dangers and elevates to the things of heaven; the means for us as it is our duty to accept our work from divine providence both in the natural as well as in the supernatural order; the means of exercising the works of charity. Finally work is the norm and the law of religious life since its origin according to the motto: Pray and work.

By the canonical name 'contemplative life' we do not mean the internal and theological life to which are invited all who live the religious life or who live in the world, and which all souls can practice, but the external profession of religious discipline which, whether by the exercise of piety, prayer, mortification, or by the occupations to which the nuns are devoted, is so ordained to internal contemplation, that the entire life and action can easily and ought efficaciously tend to contemplation." (I, 78-80)

On December 8, speaking to the delegates of the International Congress of Religious, Pope Pius XII said: "One can blend together the most laborious activity and the treasure accumulated in the interior life.... The fervor of external works and the care of the interior life not only demand mutual accord, but at least in esteem and research, it is necessary that they proceed with an equal step. Hence in the measure in which fervor for zealous works increases, there should also be an increase in faith, prayer, the desire to consecrate oneself entirely to God, the purity of a conscience without spot, obedience, patience in bearing adversities, active and vigilant charity for God and neighbor. This holds not only for religious taken individually who wish to be such, by wearing the habit and by interior dispositions, but also for the entire religious family. That is why the religious life remains on a solid foundation, before God and men, and is worthy of complete approbation.... The Church asks you, it begs you fervently, that your external activity progress in proportion to your internal life in such a way that they are both in mutual and perfect equilibrium. Did you not make profession to embrace the state of evangelical perfection? If so, bring

forth the fruits of this state in order that the mystical
body of Christ, which is the Church, by your vigor and
fervor, may attain a greater strength. This is why the
orders of the contemplative life, in a certain way, are
necessary to the Church, of which they are the perpetual
ornament and the source of heavenly graces." (IV, 321ss)

CHAPTER XII

ADAPTATION OF THE RELIGIOUS LIFE

1. NECESSITY OF SPEAKING OF THIS

Father Benjamin of the Holy Trinity, Carmelite, has written: "The great publicity that has been made regarding the problem of modernizing religious, both within each institute as well as in the press and among the faithful, seems to us to be inopportune. The faithful either misunderstand the question, or are almost scandalized, while the religious themselves, especially the young ones, easily believe that the principal purpose of their institute is at stake." (II, 188)

One might even say that similar phenomena of travesty of the truth, of pharisaical scandal, of misunderstandings and unfounded fears make necessary the treatment of this question with care.

It is evident that in view of this problem of adaptation there are among religious, in ignorance or uncertitude, in discord or expectation, two well defined currents, both badly orientated, although proceeding from opposite starting points.

The first current consists of dynamists, progression-ists, modernizers, innovators, revolutionaries, anti-conformists. They struggle for an exaggerated modernization, demanding unnecessary and useless innovations. They cry out loudly against the past and acclaim the future of which they ardently dream. Such a mentality, modernistic rather than sanely modern, which destroys without constructing, is proper especially to the young, too proud and sure of themselves. It is a sad mark of the modern age even in the field of fine arts, of philosophy, etc.

The other current consists of those who are static, con-servatives, traditionalists, archaists, anti-revolutionaries, conformists. They oppose every change. They hold in horror every innovation, because according to them the past does not need revision. Such a mentality, traditional-istic but not sanely traditional, enemy of just progress, which crystallizes and fossilizes the past, is usually met among the aged, for whom the past constitutes a part, and a very large part, of their life.

In order to clarify the ideas of all, to put the problem in its true light, it must be treated with care, using exact terms, premises and conclusions.

2. THE RIGHT KIND OF MODERNIZATION

In the complex machine of the religious life certain elements constitute the essential and immovable part; others, on the contrary, represent the secondary, acciden-tal and variable part.

Among the first must be noted the goal and the general spirit of the religious life (evangelical perfection, the goal of all souls) and the specific goal and spirit of each institute, that is, the special color, tonality and purpose that each of them has received from its founder and first disciples.

These basic elements of the religious life must be preserved. And if, in regard to them, one may and must speak of bringing them up to date, that would mean only the actual necessity of knowing them better, of esteeming the Holy Gospel and of living more intensely in its light. One must not easily give in to the temptation—to use the words of Father Golia, S.J.—"to mix water with the good wine of the religious life, to take away from it the thorns and the hedge, for the purpose of uniting the charms of liberty to a lighter and sweeter evangelical perfection." (II, 500)

Another category of elements of the religious life is composed especially of the means that the various religious institutes have at their dispositions and offer to their members to attain their proper end; material and spiritual means; means which concern the spiritual life, the government of the houses of the congregation, the external modalities of the apostolate, the work and the profession of the religious, the manner of clothing, the quality and quantity of nourishment, modern commodities, etc.

Now it belongs to instruments and means to serve and to adapt themselves to the end. They may, then, according to the changing circumstances of time and place, be replaced by means that are better adapted, or they may simply be modified. And sometimes it will be necessary to add new methods to the old ones.

An example will illustrate the principle just mentioned. It is from the late Father Suarez, Master-general of the Dominicans. "Certain things which were formerly established as a sign of poverty and mortification, today are considered as expensive and more comfortable. In the ancient constitutions of the Order of Preachers the rule was that garments should be made of cheap material, or of wool. There was an abundance of sheep in those days; wool was woven in nearly all the families, but not in the way in which it is made today. Hence one could wear garments of wool with little expense, and these crude garments were not too comfortable. Today, on the other hand, especially in certain regions, the price of wool is very high, and it is almost a luxury to wear woolen clothes, and the manner in which it is prepared makes it a garment that is comfortable and agreeable." (I, 256)

Hence it would be opposing the mind of the founder to defend at any price the letter of the law while sacrificing the spirit of poverty and mortification which dictated it, unless there be considerations of another order which justify it still today. That would be equal to placing the means above their end, which is an absurdity and an evil.

Cardinal Siri, Archbishop of Genoa, writes: "We welcome the renewal which impresses on the Orders a movement of return towards their origins, from which several have gone astray! But we reject a rejuvenation which would open the gate to vague spirituality, born of poor theology . . . which mitigates the clear concrete austerity of the gospel, made up of the cross, renouncement, charity, and union with Christ." (II, 20s)

When these same principles are admitted and when the necessary and opportune practical applications are drawn from them, one will remain at a safe distance from the two extreme currents, both worthy of reproach. Avoiding a shabby conservatism and an adventurous progressivism, one will stand on the praiseworthy basis of tradition and of a holy modern spirit.

3. RELIGIOUS LIFE AND MODERN PROGRESS

A vast field in which one can and must realize a true rejuvenation is offered by the new material means which modern progress continues to place at the disposal of men to make life more comfortable and work more fruitful.

There was a time when the question was seriously asked whether it was permissable for a religious to have two garments. Today, among actual questions it is asked whether it is permitted or not, whether it is fitting or not to use modern means such as the telephone, telegraph, radio, television, microphone, loud-speaker, movie, auto, airplanes, typewriters, conveyor, air conditioners, etc.

Here also it will be good to guard against the two extremes; introducing without discernment all these means, all these innovations into all the communities or to pronounce a categorical and universal "Non licet." At the same time it would be wrong to approve the introduction of these new inventions with the scandalized air of one who says: These are necessary evils.

For a true estimation the following principles must be retained:

a) The use of these means is not permitted in a community if it means the introduction of the superfluous, or still worse, of luxury. For example, there can be sufficient reasons for equipping a library or a laboratory with modern furniture, but there is no reason for furniture of precious wood, elegantly and expensively carved, because with less expense one can equally well attain the desired end. A camera can be necessary or very useful for the one who edits a periodical or has charge of advertising, etc., but it is often entirely useless for others. The religious house ought never to be a luxurious collection of modern apartments, equipped with every comfort.

b) Those things must be excluded which only serve to make life more comfortable and to familiarize the religious with the maxims of the world. Such would be, among so many others, air-conditioning in a country where heat or cold is easily bearable, even with a little mortification.

"The saints are our teachers," writes Father Louis of the Immaculate (Carmelite). "This program written by a young delicate girl, called by God to the religious life, might appear frightening or exaggerated: 'To keep myself at all times and circumstances ready to suffer and to be inconvenienced, never to satisfy any desire or appetite, even though the matter be small and licit; to find means to make unpleasant and mortifying for the body the simple and inevitable necessities.' Such a program is indeed very austere, but when put into practice it led to the honors of sanctity the one who made it, at the age of scarcely twenty-three years. It certainly would not have been so

if Therese Margaret Redi had sought a fuller life using—
no doubt in order not to pass as a retrograde—all the
commodities which the life of her time could offer."
(II, 43)

c) When a means, put at the disposition of the whole
community, attains the praiseworthy end which justifies
its introduction, it should not be left at the disposition
of individuals. The common good is to be preferred to
that of the individual. Thus, for example, the use of the
radio ought to be regulated.

d) To judge of the necessity or utility of modern
means for religious, one must consider other circumstances. Let us explain the principle by examples.

Where there is no road, or when it is a question of
a very long trip, one may travel by plane. This, however,
is not to be considered as the ordinary means of transportation for religious.

In time of war or general disaster, the religious also,
even before the people of the world, should adopt meas-
ures much more severe than in ordinary times, to avoid
unnecessary expenses.

In places where the standard of living is notably higher,
things are permitted to religious which would not be
permitted where misery and poverty are general.

"There cannot be," writes Father Alberione, superior
general of the Society of St. Paul, "an Italian, American,
or Asiatic sanctity. Let there be a sanctity according to
wisdom which takes into account the circumstances of
the times, places, and persons, but which always leads
to the love of God. . . . Sin is always sin; virtue is always

virtue. There is only one religious life, that which has been taught by Our Lord, founder, legislator, aid, consolation and reward of the true religious." (I, 269s)

What can be useful and even necessary for one congregation—in view of its specific end, its type of apostolate and its particular spirit—can be illicit for others. Let us consider the two extremes: an institute which has schools, laboratories, recreation courses, etc., and a purely contemplative order.

Only very particular circumstances can justify the use of more comfortable means which scandalize the people, especially the poor, for example, a personal auto instead of the public means of transportation; first class or Pullman travel in trains instead of a lower class. One can, however, envisage the extraordinary case of a religious who must make a long journey, or do some intellectual work en route, or give conferences at his arrival. In such a case one would be more generous with him.

e) A final general principle can be announced in these terms: granted that these modern means can offer advantages for health, work, etc., and inconveniences or dangers for the soul when they are abused, one must in each case calculate the pro and con and among the means equally apt to lead to an end, and let those be chosen which offer more advantages than inconveniences.

In a report made to the Congress of Religious, Father Solano of Zurich, provincial minister of the Capuchins, gives the result of an inquiry on the usages and opinions concerning the press, radio, movies and telephone in thirty religious houses of Switzerland. It is interesting to consider it. (II, 458-461)

Here is the customary usage:

1. *Daily papers*

Hardly any written norm exists; custom is the ordinary guide. The more contemplative orders, considering the papers as a necessary evil, subscribe to one or the other, leaving the matter in the hands of the superior, who from time to time may have extracts read to their subjects in the refectory or at recreation. In active congregations certain papers are taken, as means of instruction and useful information. These are at the disposition of all, and are usually placed in the recreation room or in a small library. Where the papers are allowed with restriction, they are given to the priests rather than to the lay brothers, the students or sisters. A final development has given consent even to individual religious to subscribe to papers. Moreover, here and there, although very rarely, so-called independent papers are mingled with the Catholic publications.

2. *Periodicals*

Everywhere a greater liberty is granted, whether for subscription or for the reading of religious, ascetical, and missionary periodicals; these may be read in one's cell. Even the individuals can obtain these through purchase or gift. Periodicals on the sciences or profane arts are permitted, most often only to specialists, so that they may read them during study time.

3. *Radio*

The contemplative orders are obstinate in refusing, for the most part, to admit radios in the convents. At the most, they permit them in the chaplain's quarters. On the contrary the active congregations open the door to them more easily, putting them in their schools, institutes, or hospitals, sometimes in an annex of the convent so that the religious also may hear the religious programs or special instructive programs. But the private use of the radio in the cells of the religious is nearly everywhere forbidden. In a few convents it is permitted to certain ones, usually those adept in music, the sick, the blind, etc.

4. *Movies*

The contemplative orders admit only religious films on the Saints or the missions. Some active or mixed congregations, besides having some movies within their walls, begin to frequent public movies, even those outside parish projects, if the films are religious or at least very instructive. Several congregations, especially those called active, limit the viewing of public movies to those who accompany the pupils, or at least they forbid their members from attending night movies, or forbid all pictures outside the religious house. Such communities, however, are not numerous and always in the minority. They are usually in Catholic cities where the movie directors show the better films.

5. *Telephone*

The telephone has been introduced nearly everywhere as something almost inevitable. Very few convents of nuns do not admit a telephone. Some others have placed it outside the cloister for the exclusive use of the superior and the economist. With the exception of very rare congregations of men which grant, at least to the priests, full freedom to use the telephone, nearly all the others demand a special permission. Some add the surveillance of a companion sister or the superior who might listen in on an extension.

Such are the customs.

Here are the opinions.

1. *Advantages of newspapers*

The esteem and the love of a religious vocation, the joy of living the religious life can be renewed by them. The soul, in contact with material progress, feels disposed to the necessary adaptation of the religious life. Concrete facts, often better than a good book, especially among women, encourage the practice of the virtues. Finally the soul can be led to depart from a kind of egoistic asceticism, to live in a transport of universal charity, in a spirit of reparation and prayer when it is better acquainted with the evil of the world and the sufferings of the Church.

Dangers of newspapers

Even if we suppose that only Catholic papers are read, the spirit becomes superficial and a friend of the easy life; much time is lost, which is precious for prayer and study;

the reading of books is curtailed; and gradually one de-
vours the newspapers, not with a desire of knowledge but
through curiosity. Thus the spirit is applied more and
more to the things of the world; they are spoken of in
conversation and thought of during spiritual exercises. And
thus perhaps a certain confusion is introduced into one's
ideas, especially among women, through a lack of a right
understanding of what is read.

2. *Advantages of periodicals (in addition to those mentioned when we spoke of the reading of newspapers)*

Religious periodicals bring asceticism up to date and
feed the apostolic and missionary zeal. Those which concern the arts favor activity and the pleasure of work, they
often facilitate obedience of the subjects who appreciate
the good will and liberality of the superiors.

Dangers of periodicals (in addition to those mentioned
regarding newspapers)

It is possible that they favor a certain exaggeration
in regard to novelties, or the desire of the emotions, or
the desire for things not in conformity with religious
poverty.

3. *Advantages of the radio*

According to an almost unanimous opinion these advantages are slight and can be furnished also by newspapers and other means. It can be edifying and instructive
for sisters to follow solemn religious ceremonies, to hear
pious discourses from celebrated preachers and the Holy

Father. According to the opinion of others, listening to music and other recreation programs elevates the soul and disposes it for work—and even for prayer.

Dangers of the radio

The desire to hear what one can read later in papers, hence, loss of time; a certain difficulty for the practice of fraternal charity, one listener wishing one thing, another something else; hindrance to silence, which is so necessary for tranquility and recollection; threat to the purity of faith because of certain broadcasts from non-Catholic stations; scandal perhaps of the faithful and of benefactors. It often happens that the radio ends by being a thing of annoyance and it is seldom or never turned on. In such a case its usage is easily regulated.

4. *Advantages of movies*

Good films have a particular efficacy for leading us to good. Attending good movies encourages the faithful to attend also; this favors the making, the importing and the advertising of good films and makes possible the foundation of Catholic commissions, recognized publicly, and engaged in the promotion of good movies.

Dangers of movies

The pleasure that is experienced by watching movies excites a greater desire of novelty and emotion. The spirit can be brought little by little to reason without too much consistency, with danger to the faith. The concrete life of perfection is certainly not aided by the romantic and unusual life that the movies show us.

5. *Advantages of the telephone*

Communities which carry on an external apostolate consider the telephone as indispensable. The contemplative orders see in it a slight help for the life of perfection. The greatest advantage is the saving of time, precious for prayer and study, thanks to the suppression of letters and journeys. It gives assurance in regard to the sick . . . ; and when one has a profitable business, for example a pharmacy or a laboratory, it often increases the clientele, to the great advantage of the spiritual tranquility of the religious, less preoccupied with temporal necessities.

Dangers of the telephone

Very frequent calls, at the time when the religious are in the refectory or in choir; multiplied contacts with the world, means of long conversations.

Father Kramer, C.PP.S. thus concludes his study: "An excellent weapon against the danger is complete and entire submission to the superior by means of obedience. Whoever allows himself to be guided by his own judgment . . . in things so closely bound to concupiscence, easily, even unknowingly and against his will, finds himself entangled in the love of and search for the things of this earth. Today the number and variety of material affairs that the religious must handle, constantly increase. The religious superiors, not without regret, know the peril and the danger brought to the religious life by such things as the auto and radio, as well as the difficulty of making opportune and fitting rules which allow one to keep the benefits without grave danger for poverty. In all confidence one can expect the supernatural help from God, in the measure necessary for

impeding the search for and attachment to harmful earthly
goods, on condition that they be used with care according
to the norms of reason. Material things, even if they are
not without danger, are good in themselves; they can be
of great service to the Church and the religious life. To
suppress the abuses and to regulate the uses is not easy.
That is why it is of the greatest importance to use them
in a way conformable with religious poverty. One must
pay greater attention to the manner of possession than
to the thing itself. Let those who buy be like those who
do not possess and let those who use this world be like
those who do not use it." (II, 435s)

4. OBLIGATION OF A CORRECT ADAPTATION

To save souls the only Son of God became man, like
us in all things except sin. He adapted himself thoroughly
to human frailty to lead it more easily to good and to
heaven.

For the same purpose St. Paul became all to all—
a Hebrew with Hebrews, a gentile with the gentiles, weak
with the weak, etc.—to lead them all to Christ. (I Cor.
9, 19-23)

The Church of God, while remaining the same since
its beginning until the present day, has constantly adapted
its instruments of the apostolate to the various circumstances of time and place.

The very history of the religious congregations is there
to testify that the religious life, while remaining the same
in its essential and unchangeable elements, has constantly
changed in a notable way the secondary elements, causing

new religious families to flourish throughout the ages, families that differ in many ways from the preceding ones, under the vigilant guidance of the Church, guardian and interpreter of the Gospel, eternal guarantee of truth and sanctity.

It is the law of every human being to change constantly while remaining always the same. Sclerosis or any other sickness impedes the natural adaptation and functioning of the organism, and leads it to death. No one would dream of putting the same clothes on the same individual at different periods of his life, or at different seasons of the year; of nourishing him with the same food, of subjecting him always to the same actions.

Today more than ever the will of the Church is precise and explicit concerning the congregations which it has approved, demanding that they adapt themselves, under its control, in all that is necessary and useful, to the new conditions of modern life. And the will of the Church manifested first of all by the Pope and the Sacred Congregation of Religious is also that of Christ and of God. The founders of the communities which have been most successful in corresponding to the needs of their times, did not hesitate at all to introduce changes conformable to the directives of the Church.

A final reason—but not the least—which obliges religious to adapt themselves wisely, is the rapid and ingenious modernization of the world and of the enemies of God and of His Church in the last decades. Compared to these enemies, alas! the guardians of the Father's field have slept a little, while the weeds were being sowed. But, thanks to God, our holy mother Church has sounded the alarm, calling at harvest time all the good, and in first place with the priests, the souls which are entirely consecrated to God and to His cause.

"That is why," says Father Agatangelo of Langasco, O.F.M. Cap., "that each one of us should examine himself to see if he has sought to carry out all that has been commanded by the respective authority; be prompt to receive and to carry out all that will be established by the authorities; see whether there is not something to do, on his part, that the encouragements and exhortations of the legitimate authority be promulgated and realized." (II, 17)

5. THE FITTING ADAPTATION MUST PROCEED
FROM THE SPIRIT OF FERVOR

Father Lombardi, S.J., has written: "No renewal of religious is possible if there is not a renewal in their inner spiritual life." (I, 116)

Every religious soul, by the tenor of its religious life and its contrary or favorable attitude towards a fitting adaptation, has its part of responsibility complementing the prescriptions of the superiors.

The auxiliary bishop of Lyon, Monsignor Ancel, superior general of the Priests of Prado, recalls: "It is a pernicious error to believe that only by changing the constitutions or religious observances the desired result will be obtained. It seems that certain reformers see only the juridical aspect of the problem; and certain religious souls lose their interior peace because they believe they cannot gain sanctity unless the structural reforms are made first.

In the past the Church permitted certain religious institutes the mitigation of the demands of the primitive rule in order to avoid greater evils. These dispensations were in themselves deplorable because they were signs of a lessening of fervor and the prelude of relaxation. Thus only the religious societies that are truly fervent can modernize themselves. Thus we find a new argument in favor of the primacy which ought to be accorded to spiritual renewal. It is necessary above all to procure for superiors as well as for subjects the possibility of a profound renewal of faith, hope, and charity. It is necessary to assure them the concrete possibility of uniting themselves to Our Lord, in order that in faith, which is a gift of God, they can guarantee the efficacy of their own efforts. It is good to recall the wonderful effects obtained by the preaching of the spiritual exercises at the time of St. Ignatius and his first companions. . . . But it is not sufficient to preach the spiritual exercises to obtain these results; it is also necessary that the one who preaches them be a saint. For that it would seem particularly useful in our days to choose truly supernatural preachers to consecrate them to this spiritual renewal without which the efforts of adaptation will be a miserable failure and will lead only to laxity."

"When the renewal and the spiritual equilibrium," concludes Monsignor Ancel, "are thus established in a religious society it can modernize itself by means of a better realization of its ideal of spirituality and of the apostolate. One sees gradually what should be changed in the constitutions and customs. Then one easily accepts to submit each project to the legitimate authority and especially to the supreme magisterium of the Church, for only one thing is desired: to know the will of God in order to accomplish it with the aid of His grace." (I, 123-126)

Father Larraona adds: "There is no perfection without observance, nor observance without perfection. The perfection acquired without observance would be presumptuous and chimerical; observance without a content of perfection would be vain and empty and would lead to the letter which kills, to deceiving pharisaism, to traditions which deny and obscure true tradition. Discipline and law—general and particular—are similar to the bone and muscular systems of the body. Without bone and without muscles one cannot walk. With broken bones and loose muscles one walks poorly. All agree that one cannot remain without bone or muscles." Recurring to another comparison one can say that "if there is no fire of charity, the ardor and the thirst of true perfection, the train will be all ready to go, but it will remain motionless at its point of departure."

"Perfection," writes Father Llamera, "is the theme of themes; it is the essential reason of the religious life. The religious state can be improved by making its members better. It would be a rash undertaking to pretend to give strength to the tree of the religious life by cultivating the branches and the leaves and by neglecting the roots. And the profound and eternal root of this life is a great desire of divine perfection, a vital desire for divinization, for becoming perfect as our heavenly Father is perfect. The renewal of the religious life is the only efficacious formula. It is the renewal and strengthening of the religious spirit, the indwelling of the Holy Spirit, the spirit of love, the desire and will of union with God, the search for Christian perfection." (II, 67)

Father Marie-Eugene of the Child Jesus remarks: "To show in what way such a congregation must adapt itself to the needs of the time to continue its spiritual mission, is a delicate art. The spirit of a religious order has been incarnate a first time in a founder who was ordinarily a saint. The reincarnations or thorough spiritual reforms are not less difficult. This is proved by experience. They remain one of the privileges of sanctity." (II, 33)

Father Langlais, O.P., says: "An institute is a moral person; it is also a member of the Church, a living organ of the Mystical Body of Christ. In its quality of moral person it does not live nor act; it has no influence nor merit except through the worth and sanctity of its members, of the persons who compose it. In general it is not so much the communities that have need of renewal and adaptation as the persons themselves; these must answer to the call of souls: give us saints!" (II, 208s)

6. WORDS OF THE POPE

On July 21, 1939, speaking to the Canons Regular of St. Augustine, Pope Pius XII said: "At these times a secular tradition would risk being languishing or deficient in its applications if a breath of progress and adaptation did not come to vivify it." (I, 5)

Speaking to a congregation of Cistercians on June 13, 1943 the Pope said: "Religious orders, even those noted for their antiquity, have carefully applied themselves to remove things fallen into disuse, to accomodate other

things by adaptation, and, finally to change them alto-
gether." And this is entirely to their praise because of the
"necessity to adapt the constitutions and rules, conceding
that the first conditions of their foundations have been
changed." (I, 16)

On May 8, 1947, speaking of the delegates to the chapter of the Congregation of the Holy Redeemer: "See first
of all what your solemn engagement will be: to religiously
keep and constantly preserve the things that St. Alphonsus
placed as the foundation of this society; to consider attentively, on the other hand, and examine if they ought
not to be changed in part because of the changing times
and places, the things which concern the exterior modes
of living and acting in order that the holy deposit which
has been consigned to us during such a long period of
years, might not suffer any loss or damage." (I, 23)

On the occasion of the beatification of Blessed Cafasso,
Pope Pius XII said: "Without doubt the times change,
and even the care of souls must be adapted to ever vary-
ing circumstances. . . . But beyond all the human vicissi-
tudes, the foundation, the spirit, the soul of sacerdotal life
and activity remain invariable. The lighthouse remains
immovable on the rock. Thus the life-buoy which the wave
rocks, elevates or lowers, according to its caprice, is not
a sure guide unless it is solidly anchored to a tranquil
and stable base." (I, 25)

On April 11, 1948, speaking to the Abbot General of
the congregation of St. Mary of Mount Olivet, Pope Pius
said: "Let your religious emulate one another in the most
fitting way possible, but first, order your religious life

in such a way that each of you seem to make the Blessed Bernard Tolomei relive and act again." (I, 28)

On April 30, 1949, at the Leonian College of Anagni: "If it is true that those are in error who, moved by a childish and immoderate desire of novelties, wound by their doctrine, acts, and agitations, the immutability of the Church, it is not less certain that they also deceive themselves who search, knowingly or not, to grow stiff in a sterile immobility. The Church, the Mystical Body of Christ, is, like the men who compose it, a living organism, always substantially equal to itself; and Peter would recognize in the Church of the twentieth century the first society of believers that he addressed on the day of Pentecost. But the living body increases, develops, and tends to mature. The Mystical Body of Christ, like the members who compose it, does not live nor move in the abstract, outside of the ever changing conditions of time and place. It is not and cannot be separated from the world which surrounds it. It is always of the world; it advances day by day, hour by hour, constantly adapting its way and its comportment to that of the society which is the place of its activity." (I, 33)

Exhorting the clergy of the Catholic world on September 23, 1950, Pope Pius said: "You have already noted that among priests, especially those who are poorer in doctrine and of a less strict life, restless spirit of novelty is spreading in an alarming way. Novelty by itself is never a criterion of truth; it is not worthy of praise unless it conforms to the truth and leads to righteousness and virtue." (I, 46)

On the twelfth of November, 1950, in a letter addressed to the cardinal prefect of the Congregation of Religious, on occasion of the famous International Congress of Religious: "To renew oneself and one's own goods is certainly not the same thing as to reject or despise inconsiderately all that has been laboriously accomplished by those who have gone before and who ought to be considered as the honor and ornament of the congregation. It is rather not to be made languid in an inert life, to manifest by one's own actions the great doings of one's predecessors, to cultivate intensely the flame of piety, to strive in every way and by all means in order that the holy laws of one's institute do not give the impression of a mass of external and useless rules—the letter of which, without the spirit, kills, but that they be truly so many instruments of heavenly grace. Those who use them will have a more intense desire of sanctity and will put all their efforts, according to the example of St. Paul, to procure the salvation of their brothers. If those who are consecrated to God must adapt themselves to the manners of the changing times, for no reason and in no way, must they second the demands, the foolish suggestions and the appeals of the world? But it is necessary that they be concerned with getting ahead in the way of sanctity, exploiting as much as possible all progress of the sciences and arts for the advantage of religion . . . to prefer, in the accomplishment of their efforts, these aids, which, according to the judgment of their superiors, appear more opportune, efficient and useful, whether for safeguarding the dignity of the priesthood, or for keeping religious discipline. If these principles and these norms, under the vigilant and discreet guardianship of this sacred congregation, are well understood by all and, what is of greater advantage, if they are applied with care, one can foresee a considerable increase of salutary fruit for the work of salvation." (I, 72s)

On November 21, 1950, in the apostolic constitution, "Sponsa Christi"—an example of adaptation among nuns, at the instigation of the Holy See, Pope Pius writes: "After having shown forth in their general outlines the origin and the merits of the holy institution of nuns, we come to the point where we must distinguish the proper and necessary elements which touch directly in a primary way the canonical contemplative life of nuns and their goal. To these original lineaments ... are added others, those also of great importance, which, although not necessary, by completing the physiognomy, correspond in a very opportune way to the public goal of the institution of nuns and contribute to assure it. On the other hand ... we find elements which are not of necessity, nor a complement, but only external and historical, flowing from the necessity of the times—today thoroughly changed. It is precisely these elements which, not serving any greater good, but perhaps impeding it, no longer have any reason for their existence. That is why, preserving all the principal and original elements of the institution of nuns, we have decreed that all that is external and added on, should be conformed, always with the required prudence, to the present necessities of the time, for, more than doing honor to the institution itself, that would give it a more complete efficacy." (I, 76s)

On December 8, 1950, speaking to the delegates of the International Congress of Religious, Pope Pius said: "My very dear brothers, we wish again to treat briefly the desire that the religious institutes have of adapting themselves to the new times and of uniting in a beautiful harmony the ancient and the new. If the young hear it said: 'it is necessary to live with our times,' 'we must adapt our efforts to our time' they will be inflamed with new ardor. . . .

Under a certain aspect that is right. Most often the founders of religious institutes consider their new work to face urgent particular necessities or tasks of the Church; and then they undertake works corresponding to the needs of their times. Thus, if you wish to follow the example of your fathers, behave in the same way as they did.

Study the inclinations, the judgments and habits of your contemporaries among whom you live, and if you find there something upright and good, make these precious elements yours, otherwise you will never be able to enlighten them, help them, elevate and guide them. But the Church has a patrimony which has remained integral from the beginning, which does not change with the flight of years, which adapts itself admirably to the necessities and to the aspirations of the human race: the principal part of this patrimony is the Catholic faith. . . . The goal of the religious life is also part of the same patrimony which you must, with great ardor, seek to attain in order that . . . you attain holiness . . . as well as your brethren. . . . In this same patrimony is contained another truth so sublime and important that it is considered as the only way of perfection—the renouncement of self for love of Christ. All this cannot change with time. But there are circumstances, in great number, in which you can and must adapt yourselves to the sentiments and to the necessities of men and of new times. To a great extent that has already been done, but now you are in the process of doing it in a full and entire manner by communicating your projects and resolutions to one another. That you have brought a praiseworthy renewal to your customs results from all that you do, individually or by your institute, in the schools, in the education of youth . . . in the solace afforded to human miseries, in the culture and progress of the sciences. Thus it must be admitted, and no one can deny our affirmation: that already there stands an imposing mass of works to come before the new times, in a renewed way. . . . Great prudence, however, is needed in order to receive from the world what is spoiled or ill; on the contrary give to it what you have that is good and holy and what corresponds to its best aspirations." (IV, 324-328)

Speaking to sisters engaged in education, on September 13, 1951, Pope Pius said: "And now let us speak of the religious life itself. The religious habit: choose it so it may be the expression of the natural, of simplicity, of religious modesty. . . . Then it will edify everyone . . . even modern youth. Even the norms of the constitutions, taken according to the letter and the spirit, facilitate and procure to the religious all that is necessary to her and all that she must do, in our times, to be a good teacher and educator. This shows itself also on the purely technical side. For example, today in many places sisters use a bicycle when their work calls for it. In the beginning it was something entirely new, but not against the rule. It is possible that certain details of the order of the day, certain prescriptions, which are only simple applications of the rule, certain customs which correspond to the conditions of the past, but at present are only a hindrance to the work of education, ought to be adapted to the new conditions. Let the major superiors and the general chapter take care to proceed conscientiously in this matter, with foresight, prudence, and courage. And if the case demands it, let them not omit to make the changes proposed by the competent ecclesiastical authority. You wish to serve the cause of Jesus and of His Church as the world today implores. It would not be reasonable to persist in the customs and manners which hurt this service or even render it impossible. The teaching and educating sisters ought to be so well versed in all that modern youth meets on its way and by which it is influenced, that the pupils may be able to say: 'We can go to the sister with our problems and our difficulties: she understands and helps.' "

On September 15, 1952, speaking to the general superiors: "It is exactly a year ago since we considered a series of problems which regard the good order of congregations of religious educators and their adaptation to present circumstances. Some, if not most of the suggestions that we gave then, hold also for the other congregations of religious. The experience of the past year encourages us to call your attention to the directives that we gave then. We ask you to conform yourself to them courageously when your sisters and your own experience tell you that the moment has come to take into account intelligently the custom of life as it is. We have a very special reason for speaking to you. You know that the religious orders of women are passing through a very severe crisis; we refer to the lessening of the number of vocations.

As to you, here are our recommendations: In this crisis of vocations, take care that the customs, the kind of life or the asceticism of your religious families do not constitute a barrier or a cause of failure. We wish to speak of certain customs which, if at other times they had a meaning, in another cultural atmosphere, do not have one today. They would only be obstacles to a vocation for a truly good and courageous girl. In our discourse of the past year we gave several examples of this. To return briefly to the question of the habit: The religious habit should always express consecration to God: it is the desired goal. For the rest, let the habit be becoming and correspond to the demands of hygiene. We could only express our satisfaction, when in the course of the year, we have seen that one or the other congregation had drawn some practical consequence from this proposal. To summarize: in these things that are not essential adapt yourselves as far as reason and well-regulated charity counsel.

Having said this, my dear daughters, we address to you two urgent exhortations: 1) a maternal affection towards your sisters; 2) their formation for the work which is to be theirs. Let there be nothing mean here, but be of an open spirit. Whether it is a question of education, pedagogy, of care of the sick, of artistic activities or others, the sister ought to have this sentiment: the superior makes possible for me an education which places me on an equal footing with my colleagues in the world. Give them even the possibility and the means to keep their professional knowledge up-to-date. We explained that also last year but we repeat it for the purpose of underlining the importance of this demand for their inner peace and the action of your sisters."

CHAPTER XIII

ECCLESIASTICAL CONSCIENCE

1. DOWN WITH THE BARRIERS!

Every religious soul has the right and the duty to love his own institute to which God has called him, and to strive for perfection according to its spirit and its specific goal.

But still more he has the duty of feeling himself a child of the Church, fully occupied with the interests of the Church which are those of the Divine Savior and of the heavenly Father.

If one has these sentiments, one will esteem and love every other congregation or Catholic association; one will have a sincere respect and a prompt obedience in regard to the Pope, but also in regard to the pastors and dioceses and parishes, which can reasonably expect to find a generous and precious ally in the religious soul.

Every form of particularism ought to be absolutely banned from a soul totally consecrated to God and to souls.

"Without doubt," writes Father Martinez de Antonana, "nothing is so beautiful, fruitful and conquering as team spirit: humanly it is one of the principal factors of the marvelous undertakings realized by the community. The Church praises it and favors it: it suffices to recall the privilege, the favors and exemptions that it has granted and still grants to congregations. But nothing is so harmful to the Church and contrary to the fruitfulness of the apostolate than team spirit in the bad sense of the word, that is to say, when charity gives place to egoism, when evangelic humility is supplanted by ambition and pharisaical pride— the peril of the new congregations as well as of the Orders having centuries of glory." (I, 440)

2. LONG LIVE THE POPE! OR OBEDIENCE?

The Vicar of Christ is the highest superior of all religious. They are held to obey him in virtue of the vows of obedience which binds them to the will of their immediate superiors. (Can. 499)

He is the commander in chief of the army of Christ, the visible head of the Mystical Body of Jesus. At a sign coming from him the true soldiers of Christ ought to hold themselves ready and act in all things according to his directives.

The obedience given to superiors of one's own institute is definitely obedience to the Vicar of Christ.

The exemption of submission to bishops and pastors, which in a larger or smaller measure, is accorded to many congregations, has only one clear and pleasing signification: it is that those exempt remain in a very special manner under the direct dependence of the sovereign pontiff and are especially devoted to him as "a living witness"—says Father Lombardi, S.J.—"and a very docile instrument of his episcopal power, which attains in its totality the whole universe." (I, 120s)

From the Holy Father all religious expect and receive directives concerning necessary and just adaptation, in order to rejuvenate and invigorate themselves for the glory of God and the good of souls.

"If the families of religious," adds Father Lombardi, "show themselves in some way recalcitrant against the supreme authority, they commit a grave error. They show in fact that they have lost the sense of their profession: they betray with one blow Jesus, the Church, and themselves. Urged by an inexcusable desire of freedom, they would be willing to appear in the view of the modern world as little republics, each one of which develops its own activity, chooses its own judge, neglecting this continual dependence which favors the necessary coordination; they would be cohorts, or even legions, but so mutually divided that one could rightly demand why they enjoy these privileges which do not appear justifiable except with full submission to the sovereign pontiff." (I, 121)

We must respect our holy rules and conform our life to them. "But let us not forget," says Father Lombardi, "that they are laws for us not because they have been written by a saint (no one could impose laws on us just because he is a saint); they impose an obligation because they have been approved by the ecclesiastical authority. That is why we owe to this authority (which is always living whereas the holy founders are dead) greater respect than to any constitution proper to our institutes."

If all the religious, concludes the same father, were truly convinced of all this, considering that submission to the Pope is the supreme bond, "then the sacred congregation of religious, to which the sovereign pontiff has delegated his power to a great extent, could guide them without difficulty in this great restoration." (I, 122)

3. EVERY CONGREGATION COMES FROM THE CHURCH AND LIVES FROM THE CHURCH

Father Carpentier writes on this point: "We consider the religious life in its actual condition as a gift guaranteed by the Church and we compare it to the Gospel, of which the Church is the sure interpreter. . . . The apostolic constitution 'Provida Mater' affirms that since the origin of Christianity and during all the centuries the Church has taught with security the manner of leading and ruling the life vowed to perfection. . . . Thus we have the certitude that the practice of the counsels, as it is realized today in the canonical religious life, truly corresponds to the will and teaching of Jesus and constitutes the evangelical state of perfection." (I, 161s)

"The religious," writes Father Van-Houtryve, "is a son of the Church before becoming the son of his Order. Let him maintain a wide horizon! Let the extent of his charity spread out! No collective egoism. It is in the name of the Church and for the Church that he prays, sacrifices, and works. He has two filial duties towards the Church. He must be found to be its child and show himself desirous of its sanctity, unity, and expansion. The doctrine of the Church ought to be the rule of his thoughts; he ought to have the same sentiments as the Church, and be ready to give his life for the faith of the Church. . . . Let him have a Catholic sense. This is not exaggerated love of the whole; one must not love his own truth, but the truth."

"Every congregation," adds Father Gambari, S.M.M., "is a living body which is inserted into another living body, the Church, and is composed of members who give themselves, interiorly and exteriorly, to it for this specific purpose, to anticipate the urgent and special needs of the church." From this it is seen that the "particular legislation of every congregation ought to be something vital and unifying, united to the life of the Church, of the civil society, and of the individuals." (I, 528)

Even the temporal goods of the congregations, numerous authors observe, are ecclesiastical goods, subject to the legislation of the Church. They cannot licitly be used for purely secular purposes. The superfluous ought to be given to the poor or used for pious works. The sovereign pontiff is their supreme administrator who watches over their use, demanding account of their management from the superiors who take care of these things by administrative organs depending on them.

Father Melsen, O. Carm., asks why the sacred congregation wished to unite in an extraordinary congress the religious of the whole world. His answer is this: "The congress had the intention of explaining more fully the way of perfection, of making the formation of religious more solid and their apostolate more efficacious, by means of which, with the help of God, we make the Church of God more living and ready for the struggle. If more than ordinary sacrifices are imposed on us, this results also from an extraordinary necessity of the Church. In this sense asceticism puts on an ecclesiastical character. For the Church by it and in it wishes to unite humanity to God. Sanctity is not something purely individual, so that each one can withdraw himself from it at will. Its necessity is deduced from the fact that each one knows that he is the guardian of his brothers. . . . He who loves the church loves God; its members are our neighbors so that in it there is necessarily mutual love."

4. MISSIONARY CONSCIENCE

When the consecrated soul has become conscious of its being and its action in the Church and for the Church, it feels the impetuous need of promoting the spread of the divine reign, not only in Christian lands but also in infidel and non-Catholic regions.

The soul then truly lives—as a Christian and *a fortiori* as a religious—its baptism and its confirmation, which have made it an adopted child of God and a soldier of Christ fully consecrated then to the increase of the family of the children of the heavenly Father and to the peaceful and salutary victories of the army of the Redeemer, Jesus.

Then only can it say that it truly loves God and the God-man in the creatures of the Lord and in the souls bought by the adorable blood of the divine crucified.

Then it will truly imitate the Missionary of the Father and the heavenly army of missionaries who have given to the Catholic missions their spirit, their heart, their life itself.

5. THE WORDS OF THE SECRETARY OF THE
SACRED CONGREGATION OF RELIGIOUS

At the time of the congress of the religious, Father Arcadius Larraona, C.M.F., was secretary of the Sacred Congregation of Religious. Showing briefly some of the more important and significant desires of these solemn sessions of religious, he began with that which concerns the love of the Church.

"The congress wished," he said, "to renew solemnly and repeatedly the sacred bond or knot of special and total obedience which attaches all the religious congregations and each of its members to the Vicar of Christ. . . . It is a consolation for us to recall that the true founder of our institutes is the Pope, who by his administrative power erected them and by his magisterium approved them. . . . Once founded and approved, the Vicar of Christ does not abandon them, for it is he who reserves to himself supreme interior power deriving from the vow . . . or from this equivalent bond, that jurisprudence demands from societies without vows and from secular institutes. . . . Continuing our traditions and faithful to our mission, we shall always have living in us the filial sense of the bonds, which attach us to the Church, in its unity, catholicity, apostolicity, and especially sanctity. Always and in all things, with the Church, obeying the orders of the Pope." (IV, 294s)

Afterwards the orator alluded to the necessity of reconciling the love of his congregation with the love of the Church:

"Holy Church," he said, "loves the splendid variety of its congregations, societies, and institutes of perfection. It desires with a maternal zeal that all these families remain faithful to their spirit, to their proper goal, to the different modalities of this apostolate. The durable actuality of communities is found in the necessity, felt even more vividly, of a total devotion to God and to the Church. Complete gift which profits from all the natural and supernatural riches of souls; which does not call for subjects cast in the same mold; which rejects with a firm hand all that is not pure, right and worthy, but in purifying, elevates and renders integrally supernatural what is the strength and gift of God. Fidelity to this end, to the spirit, to special orientation, signifies the living continuation of the work of the founders. The lasting and ever new reasons for which the Church has erected and approved the societies of perfection.... The congress has underlined energetically the profound and substantial unity of the life of perfection and of the apostolate in the ineffable and divine variety, in the marvelous riches of its forms. It is necessary to make living in a practical way this unity in variety, this variety in unity, eliminating with a firm conviction and a spontaneous generosity all that separates, divides, confounds; and searching, on the contrary, all that unites and effects fraternity in the rough combats for perfection in the merciless battle against the enemies of God." (IV, 301, 305)

6. WORDS OF THE POPE

Addressing the Jesuits on April 27, 1941, Pope Pius XII said: "To think, to feel, to act with the Church, and with the Vicar of Christ—for four centuries—this was the duty and the merit to which the Ignatian family consecrated its life and remained faithful, immovable in the catastrophes even when, amidst the evil of the times, the envy of the world, the horrors of the tempest, the supreme paternal hand immolated them to the tranquility of the boat of Peter. Faithful in misfortune, it was and remained such—unchangeable but conscious of the changes and of the novelties of the hour—it resumed this vigor which, bringing it back to its youth and to the maturity of the past, it was assured of a future not less fruitful in merits and sacrifices, in its unswerving devotion to the Holy See." (I, 9)

On June 13, 1943, Pope Pius wrote to a congregation of Cistercians: "The religious families, especially the monastic, raised up providentially by God according to the needs of the times, for the ornament and honor of our holy Mother Church, were resplendent like lamps with the outstanding monuments of their piety and of their activity ... offering examples of virtue to the faithful." (I, 15)

In the apostolic constitution (November 21, 1950) we read: "The perfection of the Christian life, consisting especially in charity and the charity by which we love God above all things and all others in Him, being in the concrete one and the same, our Holy Mother demands, from all the nuns who canonically make profession of the canonical life, a perfect love of God as well as a perfect love of neighbor. By virtue of this charity and of their state it is necessary that religious feel completely consecrated to the necessities of the Church and of all the needy." (I, 79)

"Loyal and faithful in an exemplary way, act so that your actions correspond to your name and that your conduct be in conformity with your profession. According to the word of the apostle 'be desirous of preserving unity of spirit in the bond of peace.' Let peace reign in you and among you, among the members of the same house and the same institute, and with those who pertain to other communities, between you and all the others who work with you to lead men to Christ. Let rivalries and discord be far from you, because these enervate and weaken and cause the most promising enterprises to fall. 'The Church, such an unlimited field of the apostolate, has an immense extent; no one will lack work and fatigue.'" (Talk to delegates to International Congress of Religious, December 8, 1950) (IV, 330s)

"How could the Church, during recent times, fulfill its mission without the work of hundreds of thousands of religious who devoted themselves, without counting the cost, in the domains of education and charity? How could the Church accomplish its mission in our days? . . . May the devotion, the love, and the sacrifices that you offer, usually in a hidden way, for the love of Christ and the good of youth bring forth fruit a hundredfold, in the future as well as in the past. May God reward you and pour out upon you an abundance of His divine favors! . . . May natural advantages, authority of the person, riches, political power, or other similar motives never lead you to deny your ideal of education, nor make you unfaithful to your mission. This paternal exhortation is provoked only by our benevolence for you, for your cares are also ours, your happy success also. To reach a result so enviable harmony and generous concord between religious families can contribute much. Reciprocal knowledge, mutual encouragement and a holy emulation can only be a strong advantage for you. Excellent beginnings have already appeared, you need but continue." (Address to Congress of Religious, September 13, 1951)

Speaking to Mothers-general, September 15, 1952, Pope Pius said: "You come, dear daughters, from all parts of the world, from far and near. Tell your sisters that we thank them for their prayers which we need so much; for their good example, which greatly aids so many Catholics in their faith and which draws to the church such a great number of those who do not belong to it. For the sisters' work in the service of the young, of the sick, of the poor, in the mission and in so many other ways, is precious for the increase and spread of the reign of Jesus in souls. Tell your sisters we have for them the greatest affection; that their preoccupations are ours, their joys also; that we wish them especially the double strength of courage and patience, in the pursuit of their own perfection and in the apostolate that their divine Master and Spouse has confided to them."

CONCLUSION

We are pleased to close this work with these warm and moving words which Father Arcadius Larraona addressed, as a final, fraternal greeting to those attending the congress.

"Obeying the sweet invitation of the call (if you wish to be perfect) we have followed Jesus, Who in His merciful love draws us.

Through love and with love we have promised Him great things ... the Lord Himself has promised us still greater things. ...

An apostolic sanctity, informed by charity and supported by all the divine and human virtues, all the gifts and actual graces that love tends to change into life by changing life—our whole life or that of others—into divine and eternal love!

A holy and continual apostolate which manifests sanctity but at the same time feeds it and develops it! ...

He, the Lord, Who called us, is our reward and our most gracious glory! We shall have Him at the same time as all those whom we have loved, saved, sanctified by example, prayer, sacrifice and action.

All that is enclosed in the fruitful seed of our vocation.

We have believed, we do believe, we cannot cease to believe in the charity of God, Who is love.

Because of our fidelity may the Lord believe and with Him, all the children of God, in the sincere practice of our love. Thou knowest, O Lord, that I love Thee and all others in Thee.

May the crowning of our congress be the liturgical chant which opened it: 'The love of Christ has united us.'

May the gentle hearts of Jesus and Mary, to whom we have solemnly consecrated ourselves while renewing our profession, bless us!" (IV, 345s)